THE
EVERYDAY
STOIC

THE
EVERYDAY
STOIC

Simple rules
for a good life

William Mulligan

MICHAEL JOSEPH

PENGUIN MICHAEL JOSEPH

UK | USA | Canada | Ireland | Australia
India | New Zealand | South Africa

Penguin Michael Joseph is part of the Penguin Random House group of companies
whose addresses can be found at global.penguinrandomhouse.com

First published 2024
004

For text sources see page 285

Set in 13/17.75pt Garamond MT Pro
Typeset by Jouve (UK), Milton Keynes
Printed and bound in Great Britain by Clays Ltd, Elcograf S.p.A.

The authorized representative in the EEA is Penguin Random House Ireland,
Morrison Chambers, 32 Nassau Street, Dublin DO2 YH68

A CIP catalogue record for this book is available from the British Library

ISBN: 978–0–241–64329–7

www.greenpenguin.co.uk

We all deserve to flourish. It's only fair if we all get a chance to learn how to live better, for ourselves and for the people we love.

While writing this book, I received my greatest blessing in life—my daughter, Zelda.

To my wonderful partner Merci, thank you for everything you have done for our daughter, for the struggles and pain you've been through, for your unconditional love, for encouraging me to delve deeper into myself for my writing, and for fostering authenticity in this book.

This book is also dedicated to my mother, who introduced me to philosophy, and to all of my siblings – Joe, Jordan, Luke, Daniel, Erin, Niamh – and the entire Mulligan brothers team who are on this journey with me to inspire change.

A heartfelt thank you to all the strangers along the way who showed me kindness; your impact is greater than you could ever imagine.

To you, reading this book: I hope to help you become the best version of yourself.

Contents

Welcome to Stoicism

The waves were high on the wine-dark sea, and the weather was getting worse. The ship, laden with valuable cargo, tumbled about the waters, smashing with enormous force against the rocks until the hardwood hull could take no more. With terrible noises of crunching and tearing, the ship broke apart, and the cargo was lost to the bottom of the Aegean Sea.

Somehow, the owner of the cargo survived. Battered and half-drowned, Zeno, a previously wealthy merchant now made penniless, made his way into the city of Athens, and visited – as you would after surviving a shipwreck – a bookshop. There, he didn't despair about his money having entirely vanished in one bad sea trip but fell into conversation with the bookshop owner about the latest philosophical teachings.

Perhaps stunned by being the sole survivor of the wreck, and being surrounded by intense debates around existence, Zeno began to develop his own philosophy. His followers came to be known as Stoics after the Stoa Poikile, the covered walkway in the public space of ancient Athens where they met each day. (Stoicism was originally called Zenonism, but they swiftly switched away from naming it after their teacher in recognition that any teacher would be flawed and it could potentially develop the philosophy into a personality cult). After Zeno's death, the next Stoic leader was Cleanthes, a water carrier and boxer known as 'the ass' for his strength and patience; then Chrysippus, a long-distance runner and prolific writer. Chrysippus's many written works were a key factor in the spread of Stoicism, and his death was pretty enviable – he died laughing, heckling a donkey eating figs. Some time after him came Posidonius, an athlete, astronomer, mathematician and politician, who travelled across Europe and Africa and calculated the circumference of the Earth and the effect of the Moon on tides. His acclaim brought figures from around the world to his Stoic school.

Around a hundred years later was Epictetus, the scholar who obtained his freedom from enslavement despite a physical disability, and who turned Stoicism from a discursive theory into a practical way of living. He so objected to theoretical teaching that he refused to write anything down – everything we have of his lessons comes from an enthusiastic student who took notes that are still coming in handy two thousand years later, in the form of both the *Discourses* and *Enchiridion*. Epictetus was referenced by the founder of cognitive behavioural therapy as being one of the primary influences on the tool.

Our final major Stoic figure is Marcus Aurelius, the last great emperor of Rome and the philosopher king, who struggled with his own sickness through-out his life and dealt with plague, wars and the deaths of his many children. He kept personal notes on the subject of Stoic philosophy and his life within it, purely for his own self-improvement, but the text was at some point published and has continued to be shared ever since. It's still one of the key texts of

Stoicism, containing hundreds of pages of wisdom, struggle, learning and debate.

In the subsequent years, Stoicism grew to have many acclaimed followers in ancient Greece and Rome, and soon spread far beyond those countries and their captured lands, even through the rise of Christianity when many other philosophies were suppressed. Its belief in building a path to a 'good' life, in growing your character, and living in a good state of mind daily, travelled around the world and across many different cultures.

Throughout the thousands of years of Stoicism, many Stoic philosophers have suffered for their beliefs: the emperor Domitian exiled all philosophers from Rome, including the Stoic leader Epictetus, and Domitian's father Vespasian had previously gone one better and exiled specifically Stoic philosophers for corrupting their students with 'inappropriate teachings'. Musonius Rufus was held in such suspicion for his Stoic beliefs in Nero's court that he was exiled not once but twice.

But none of the Stoic philosophers ever stopped teaching Stoicism, believing that passing on these life lessons was more important than maintaining their own existence. Once you discover more about what Stoics value in life, it's hard to avoid the idea that those in power don't really like it when citizens start to say, 'Maybe we don't need to buy so much or fight each other so much for our own little bit of power.' People who are content and unafraid might become harder to influence if you've only got fear and consumerism to do it.

But Stoicism has lasted so long for one key reason: it's practical. This means several things – the fact that Stoicism is a philosophy of living means that it's flexible. There's no point in having rigid lines about what to eat or who is in the out group or what actions are forbidden if you accept that people live in wildly different circumstances and situations. It also means that it's accessible: you don't have to study millions of words, or disappear from society, to understand the philosophy and begin living a Stoic life. In fact, some of the most Stoic people I know have never even heard of it, let alone studied it. And these aspects mean that Stoicism is incredibly appealing. You can start it today, and you'll find an improvement in your life today. It delivers exactly what it offers, and the whole philosophy is about practising daily. You don't become more Stoic as you follow that path, leading to a peak Stoicism you achieve. Instead, you build good habits that make good choices easier, which leads to happiness for you and, with you developing more patience, empathy and wisdom, a better time for those around you. It's all about giving ourselves the chance to start those tiny good habits, to make a decision about how we want to live in the world and to put them together to find Stoic flourishing.

Whether we would necessarily use the word, we still all have our own philosophy. Maybe it's about how we treat people and allow others to treat us, maybe it's a wider view of the shape of the world. However we express it – or don't – we each develop a philosophy about our lives, a theory of behaviour, which shapes how we choose to live.

Zeno didn't invent something new with Stoicism – he tapped into a set of universal truths about people, how we behave, what we like and don't like, and what makes us thrive and flourish in any situation. Each chapter addresses one of those universal truths that perhaps we've lost sight of, and I hope each one brings some of that contentment and happiness from Stoicism to you.

This is a practical guide to life. There are philosophy books that will make you ask questions about existence, belief, morality and self, but this book isn't a scholarly study of theory or a dense history. It's designed to be a daily template for living a life with more peace, more happiness and in a world that's better for everyone – fairer, calmer, wiser and more enjoyable. This is about giving you the tools to be the best, happiest version of yourself. I don't want to gate-keep Stoicism; I want this book to show everyone how simple, accessible and joyful the Stoic philosophy is. Stoicism isn't about studying for exams with hundreds of books. In fact, some of the most Stoic people in the world might never even have heard of the philosophy. Stoicism is about living in a way that improves life for all, not just the few who have the financial or time resources to live 'well'. And that's the key: it's all about living.

I hope you enjoy the book, and then go out and enjoy your Stoic life.

Day by day, what you choose, what you think,
and what you do is who you become.

———

HERACLITUS

CHAPTER 1

What's Wrong with My Life, Anyway?

or How Stoicism Can Make
Everything Better

Maybe you wake up happy every morning and put your head on the pillow at the end of the day feeling fulfilled, pleasantly tired, and immediately fall into a blissful rest, readying yourself for the next day of joy. Perhaps you never have a disagreement with a friend or colleague, never experience stress in a long queue, and have never minded the end of a relationship or the loss of a job. Maybe you're the kind of person who sees every glass as not just half-full but overflowing.

In which case, congratulations. You probably don't need to read this book.

But for the rest of us, life can sometimes feel like it's just one thing after another. From the tiny complaints – a missed bus, a car out of petrol, a friend cancelling on you, an extra meeting when you'd cleared your calendar – to the big challenges of life – separation, unemployment, death – life in the twenty-first century is an endless list of emotional, financial, mental and life tasks, all buried under the pressures and pulls of social media and an endlessly connected internet society.

We don't earn enough, we don't eat right, we don't look or dress how we should, we don't have enough friends and, if we do, we aren't doing the right things with them. Our homes should be better, our jobs should be better, we should be monetising our hobbies and performing self-care at all times, and we should be engaging in every bit of news so we can be informed and prepared for everything that might happen.

It's exhausting.

With the current pace and stresses of the world, it doesn't seem like learning to not care about a missed bus could make that much of a difference. There are such big issues in the world! Why does it matter if you can shrug off someone pushing in ahead of you at the supermarket?

But the strange truth is that those tiny little releases do make a difference. Our lives are made up of moments – right now, your current moment is sitting here, reading these words. Other tiny moments make you feel better, or worse, and enough negative moments on the wrong kind of day can make you feel that the whole day has been ruined, or whole month, whole year. On the wrong kind of day, after a few tiny bad events on previous days, it can feel like this entire thing is just too much.

But imagine living a life where those tiny things don't get to you. And where you build up such good habits around the tiny things, that when the big things come around, you're already used to thinking differently about them. About what you can control, and what you can't. About the inevitability of death, and the preciousness of life. About the footprint you want to leave in the world, and among other people. About how easily you can find happiness, if you know how to look for it.

There have been times in my life when I've struggled. Big struggles and small struggles, but all of them felt heavy and overwhelming, shaping me first into an unhappy and anxious teenager, and then an adult who was worn down, negative and angry. I struggled so much with shyness and anxiety, worrying incessantly about how to exist and help those around me, but always paralysed by fear and my own thoughts. I'd cross the road to avoid friends and not turn up to events because I'd been overthinking about what I'd said or what I could say. It cost me friendships, jobs and opportunities. I stopped eating, stopped sleeping and became a prisoner of my own limitations. Every self-help book I read at the time seemed to be written by someone brimming with confidence, who always had the answers, who never doubted their success, and seemed a million years from where I was.

*

Then I discovered Stoicism.

Or, more specifically, my mum introduced me to Stoicism. She was a single mum raising seven children by herself, and a nurse with short pink hair. She is still the strongest person I've ever known.

I was working as a building-site labourer at the time, commuting four hours a day for a small wage in a job I didn't love, for a boss I didn't get on with. I'd ask him to at least pay me minimum wage and he'd refuse, saying if I really wanted more money I'd work every weekend, instead of just most of them. It felt like my life was slipping away, and every day I was feeling like my plans for the future and my ambition were being drained out of me. Then Mum gave me a book. I'd never been much of a reader before, but she pointed out I had all that time to kill on buses every day, so if it didn't make me travel sick, why not spend it reading? At the time a nurse, my mum had previously run a drug rehabilitation centre, so many of her books were about recovery, addiction and psychology; an unusual range to start a new reader on. But I slowly moved from one book to another, choosing things from her overflowing bookcase, and began to discover worlds I'd never dreamed of, voices I'd never imagined. I realised one day that I no longer saw those four hours as a waste of my life, but as a gift I was being given that other people might have been desperate for. A curse had been turned into a blessing.

One day, when I was waiting in the early morning for my bus, a bin man came over and held a book out to me. I must have looked confused, so he explained that he always saw me reading there in the mornings and had spotted this book lying on top of a bin and kept it for me. He didn't say anything else, just accepted my thanks and went on his way. I didn't see him again, but that small gesture from a stranger shifted something in my head. Was it possible that people weren't always potential threats? Could it be true that most people wanted to do good things for others around them?

Eventually, I came to Marcus Aurelius's *Meditations*. At first glance, it seemed an impossibly dense read for someone who'd barely opened a book a year before – a two-thousand-year-old philosophical journal, originally written in ancient Greek? But as I began reading, it quickly became clear that the writing was fascinating and completely relevant to my life and the lives of those around me. I remember one passage I read, where Marcus Aurelius wrote of his goal to be 'like the rock that the waves keep crashing over. It stands unmoved and the raging of the sea falls still around it.' I lived in such turbulence and uncertainty that the mental image of being still and certain in an unstable world made me stop completely, and gave me a small hope that my future could look different to anything I'd imagined before. The more I read, the more I was surprised that this acclaimed historical figure, last of the great Roman emperors, was just a human like me – worried about his family, his temper, his confidence, his colleagues. He may have led wars and run an empire, but his main concern was how he could be the good man he wanted to be, finding a strength through kindness, fairness and care for others.

Stoicism seemed to, if not answer every question, then start me asking questions about how to live and die so the world can be better for us all. It spoke about honesty and connection, self-improvement and simplicity, choice, strength and truth.

I look back now at some of the ways I behaved, how I felt, how I would react to situations, and it feels like a different person. I would be paralysed about going into shops, unable to speak to friends, would miss out on parties, would be silent at school. I was a shadow, anxious and terrified, often unable to do the simplest thing. But the Stoic philosophy made me think differently about everything, including my underpaid, overworked labouring job. I'd felt such a loyalty to my boss despite his behaviour – perhaps because of fear of an unknown alternative – but Stoicism finally made me quit my job and start on the path to what I really wanted.

My life changed then. Growing up, the seven of us were raised by my mum on her own, and there were debt collectors banging on the door. We'd always escaped into films, watching not just the films themselves but the behind-the-scenes extras about the filming and background work, following everything we could about how films were made. Now, I set up a business with my brothers, making films to help improve people's lives, with dreams that the three of us would take on Hollywood.

Soon, we had an office in our mum's attic, an area that was more of a crawl space full of Christmas decorations. It was also the bedroom of me and another brother, with bright pink fibreglass insulation bursting out of the rafters, and with no space to stand up even at the tallest point under the roof. We saved every penny from our labouring jobs to buy the computers to work on and set up Mulligan Brothers, a media company with the sole purpose of inspiring change. We had multiple fans running in the summer to try and keep the computers from overheating and spent the winters working and sleeping up there in several layers of coats and gloves – but my brothers and I had our minds set on our plan. As we worked, I read everything I could about the Stoic philosophy, before gradually seeing it, month by month, day by day, bring me greater happiness and contentment. (When the company was finally a success, we clubbed together to buy our mum her house in an attempt to thank her for everything she'd done for us.)

One of the most interesting things about Stoicism is the idea that it's about practical habits, simple aspects that can be built on day by day to create a virtuous circle – the more we access the ideas of Stoicism, the easier we find it to react in ways that leave us feeling good and make the rest of the world around us feel better too. Far too often, we continue with the known difficulties in our lives – relationships that aren't right, jobs we are miserable in, friendships that bring us down – because we don't know if we can make the correct choices to steer our lives into a better situation. Sometimes we need to be forced into change to discover better lives, and if our lives haven't objectively improved, Stoicism offers the opportunity to discover and build resilience, optimism, perspective, wisdom and joy.

Doesn't that sound like it's worth a try?

IN SUMMARY

Stoicism is about building practical habits.

Just starting it will bring new enjoyment to your life.

One isn't necessarily born with courage, but one is born with potential. Without courage, we cannot practise any other virtue with consistency. We can't be kind, true, merciful, generous or honest.

———

MAYA ANGELOU

CHAPTER 2

Here Are the Basics

or The Four Virtues

We'll talk a lot about the Four Virtues in this book – Wisdom, Justice, Courage and Moderation – but first we need to clarify all of their various meanings and interpretations that are open to a Stoic. The Virtues are the foundation for everything a character should be, the tried-and-trusted guide for us to be a good person, and the very basis of Stoicism. Stoics understand that if we prioritise these values, we can't really go wrong – if we're wise, just, courageous and moderate, it's hard to imagine how we could be existing in a destructive or unhappy way, because the Virtues breed contentment and this contentment encourages more of the Virtues.

It's vital to have this foundation, because whether we name it or not, we all have a subconscious grounding for how we think, behave, approach others. If we don't base our foundations on some kind of moral philosophy, we'll be handed a basis for living by pop culture, social media, people we might only see a small part of in passing, and we end up prioritising possessions, presentation, accumulation. Our desires can also be influenced by and inherited from our parents – even with the best will in the world, often they impress upon us that our desires 'should' be the same as theirs, that we should wish to follow in their footsteps: many children, for instance, are raised to go into the family business. But as children are increasingly exposed to the internet from younger and younger ages, online images are having more influence than their parents, even before they've reached their teens. The influence of those images, the attractiveness of money and attention, then embed deeply in their brains and subconscious. We can copy what we see online to gain the same attention, but it provides no real framework for how to actually live, or how to thrive in society in a way that benefits everyone – when we aren't being photographed, or styling and curating the images, how do we really live? How do we conduct ourselves in difficult situations? How do we exist on our own, in a room behind a closed door, with no cameras or phones? How do we think, in the space of our own heads?

The Four Virtues offer guidance for any situation, and we can look to them to discover the most beneficial action.

EXERCISE

This is called Virtue Modelling, and it's something that's popular in many different religions and philosophies. You might have seen people wearing a WWJD bracelet – the Christians who wear them ask themselves, 'What would Jesus do?' in difficult situations.

Think of the people you know – either in real life or characters in films or books – who might reflect the Four Virtues. You don't have to think of one person who carries all four,

---

but maybe you can think of four people, each of whom carries one of the Virtues. Maybe it's someone in your family, a teacher, a friend, a colleague. Maybe it's someone in fiction, or a figure like David Attenborough or Rosa Parks. Build a clear mental picture of them around each chosen Virtue, thinking how they'd speak, react or carry themselves.

Next time you find yourself in difficulty, find some space in your mind and ask yourself: what would your chosen person do right now? How would they speak? Can you reflect their Virtue in the moment through this modelling?

If virtue promises good fortune, peace of mind and happiness, certainly also the progress towards virtue is progress towards each of these things.
— EPICTETUS

Epictetus understood that the path is as important as the destination, if not more so. Merely striving towards virtue benefits us; Stoicism is never about achieving or not achieving perfection, but about practising the habits of the Virtues, and seeing the benefits they bring to all around us when we act on those choices. Wisdom, Moderation, Courage and Justice can feel like abstract concepts – how do I wake up in the morning and practise Wisdom? – but the progress towards them brings more concrete feelings we can recognise as positive and achievable: happiness, honesty, generosity.

In ancient Greece, one of the ways the Virtues were depicted was as a tetramorph, an image of four animals signifying each Virtue – a man for Wisdom, a lion for Courage, an eagle for Justice and an ox for Moderation. But even thinking about what we, in the modern world, may or may not associate with each animal, do we understand what further ideas we can connect to each Virtue?

*

Wisdom, for example, can also mean a good calculating mind, a quick wit, discretion, subtlety, resourcefulness and plain good sense. It is the ability to recognise what is and isn't within our power, what is good and bad in the world, and functions as the cornerstone of the Four Virtues. If we know what helps us flourish, we understand better our own natures and what benefits the wider world around us. And Stoicism doesn't consider Wisdom as a binary – it's not that there are people born wise and people born foolish, and that's how we stay forever. As with any Virtue, or indeed any skill, Wisdom can be practised and improved. And why wouldn't we want to improve a skill? It all begins with practice, with understanding Wisdom and the meaning of the Virtues, and letting them guide our actions.

Like any new skill, the start is always the trickiest – but also the part where we learn the most. Development only ever comes from challenge. We judge ourselves by our internal monologue and intentions, but judge others by their external actions and behaviour. We all know that when we've done something 'wrong', we've had an excuse, or at least a reason, for doing it that way. We were stressed, we were misunderstood, we were helping someone else out. But when someone else performs a 'wrong' action, all we judge them by is what we can see. We don't know the justifications and internal conversations that have led them to that act, so our judgement is often harsh and perhaps entirely unjust. Similarly, our perceived image of someone is not the same as their moral standing. Someone with an 'aggressive walk', a rougher way of talking or scruffier clothes isn't automatically a bad person, but we've been primed by capitalism to understand the symbols of social status as being the same as moral status. Think of bankers making billions off the rest of society in economic crashes across the Western world – their manners of speech, clothes, cars, houses, all message to us that they must actually be OK people, who are just using the system as it's been designed to exploit people for their own profit. It's not their morals, it's an issue with the system! Contrast this with benefit claimants, a group consistently demonised by the press. And these are people on the whole legitimately claiming funds to keep themselves and their families housed and fed – they are using the system as it's been designed, because our system doesn't otherwise allow them to survive. But these people must be weak morally, and probably corrupt too, because look at their clothes, their speech, their homes! We've lost sight of objective Wisdom when it comes to class divides in our society.

How many times have you seen someone loudly proclaiming a moral stance on a social position online? Maybe it's an Instagram caption or an ethical battle on Twitter, yet they'll start a fight with someone taking actual steps to provide for a charity or vulnerable group because that person hasn't used the exact right wording. I have a friend who helps animals and has been a vegan for fifteen years, and recently he had this very experience commenting on someone else's post online. The person had put up footage of a cow being manhandled by a farmer, and my friend observed that worse happens all the time to factory-farmed animals. He was swiftly crushed by an avalanche of commenters, telling him he was the worst, he was evil, how could he hate animals so much – the usual calm and rational online discussion from internet debaters. He was so baffled how he, someone who has cared for the welfare of animals for a long time, trying to make a point about the lack of welfare in much of farming, could be told by meat-eating strangers online that he was somehow the problem in the world because his words were performatively wrong over the others' internet grandstanding.

An activist from a council estate may not be using today's correct terminology, but when they start a group for local young carers, they'll be doing a lot more good in the world than someone behind a keyboard whose only 'action' is to fight someone online about their vocabulary. Word trends change constantly, but making someone else feel better about themselves and their lives can have positive ripples far beyond our imagining. The keyboard warrior's only legacy is putting more disagreement into the world.

The truth is that people with good, positive thoughts who consider themselves to be 'good people' can perform 'bad' acts. Through selfishness or ignorance, they may act in a way that brings great harm to the world, but because their internal monologue is gentle and moral, they believe that they are still good people. Similarly, people with negative, harsh thoughts might be performing positive actions in the world daily, but because their internal monologue is so critical and gloomy, they struggle to see themselves as anything other than bad people. But from the outside, their footprint on the world is the opposite of how they see themselves: the 'bad' people would be seen as good, and vice versa. Our internal speech and our inner justifications are, ultimately, meaningless, and we require Wisdom to understand that reality. The actions are key, not the thoughts, the reasoning or the self-image. Remember Marcus Aurelius's famous instruction to himself: 'Waste no more time arguing what a good man should be. Be one.'

Moderation also incorporates modesty, self-control and good discipline. We can sacrifice ourselves in service of Wisdom and Courage, avoid greed and vanity, take an honest look at what we truly need, and limit our wants to those things that our reasonable judgement decides. Moderation is not simply self-discipline where we choose to exercise it – doing three hours at the gym just so we can justify eating too much junk food that makes us feel worse isn't Moderation. Dedicating ourselves to working longer hours so we can achieve more in our jobs at the cost of relationships with family and friends isn't Moderation; staying on the sofa for an entire weekend and not stepping outside for fresh air or to visit friends after a hard week at work isn't Moderation. The middle path might not be easy to find at first, but as with all Stoicism, the more we practise, the simpler our choices and our decisions become.

I remember when I first started working with my brothers, how I felt I had to work all the time. It seemed like good self-discipline to be ploughing all my time and energy into this business we'd dreamt about for so long, that if it was something I really wanted then I had to work hard for it. It didn't take long, though, for me to realise that I was exhausted and inefficient. I wasn't supposed to sacrifice everything else – friendships, relationships, fitness, sleep – but instead to find a path of Moderation. Once I realised that, it was easy to be more aware of the balance I needed in any situation: sometimes it was a day of hard work and exercise, at other times I needed to relax with friends and not think about work at all. Everything in life is better with balance.

Courage includes the habits of cheerfulness, endurance, confidence, industriousness and maintaining moral principles, making the space in your mind to face your own fears and to carry and manage difficult feelings, including hunger, pain or tiredness. When

Musonius Rufus, the teacher of Epictetus and a great Stoic philosopher, was exiled by the emperor Nero to the harsh island of Gyaros, he celebrated the practice the island offered him to hone his Stoic principles and enjoy the occasional company of fellow philosophers there. Not that you need to find a remote desert island to find your inner Stoic courage – but it doesn't hurt to remember that fear does a greater harm to us than almost anything we actually fear, and Courage removes both the fear that can paralyse us and the pain of carrying it. We know that we can be manipulated by forces outside ourselves, and one of the most powerful of these is fear. When we're watching the news and being told over and over that the world is a terrible place filled with our potential enemies, it's easy to feel panic and respond irrationally. But Courage stops us feeling lost and overwhelmed, gives us back our clarity and perspective, and points us in the right direction. Building a habit of Courage means we can behave courageously even in the face of hardship, and the more we do it, the more automatic it becomes. It's a valuable Virtue to practise.

As children, we lack so much understanding, experience and ability. When we are overwhelmed or need to express ourselves, often it can only come out as untamed, out-of-control shouting and crying. As we grow older, we (mostly) learn that calmer communication gets us what we need far better, and we use our experience and wisdom to develop our reactions. So, why don't we have that same emphasis on development away from fear? As I've grown older, I've tried to use reason to remove myself from the fear that would keep me from talking to people, going out, trying new things. Courage is required to defeat fear and a truly wise Stoic knows that however useful fear may have been in our evolution, fear is less useful as a way to teach us how to behave in society.

Finally, **Justice**, which though it might bring to mind the idea that we have the responsibility to somehow introduce a legal system into our daily lives, can also signify the ideas of honesty, fairness, equity, piety and fair dealing. Far more achievable, perhaps. In our day-to-day existence, we can easily strive to help others, do good, aim for a common benefit to all (picking up rubbish, for instance), work towards kindness and fairness and avoid anger. By developing the habit of fairness and help to all, we improve our own lives immeasurably. Think what a weight you lift from yourself if you automatically go to help those you consider your enemy. Soon, you wouldn't even have any enemies (whether or not they feel the same, the issue will have been removed from your own mind). Stoics believe that Justice is the *most* important of all these Virtues, since without Justice we're only serving ourselves (although Maya Angelou might disagree).

Looking at these Virtues now, do they seem more reachable? Can you already see how many of them you manage in your life already?

*

Another way of considering them is as the functional, foundational aspects of Stoicism. If you don't have a foundation to base your actions and reactions on, someone else will provide one and dictate how you should be in the world. These Virtues aren't merely concepts, but the behavioural tools for living Stoically:

— **Wisdom** is essential to know what is and isn't in our power, and what is good and bad in the world.
— **Courage** is essential to act on our knowledge and wisdom.
— **Justice** is essential to share and spread the Four Virtues and the philosophy of Stoicism.
— **Moderation** is essential to maintain our practices and our habits.

They stand together like the four legs of a chair, keeping Stoic habits stable, steady and functional. And they also provide details of the Four Vices, those behaviours and choices we should be avoiding in our lives:

- **Foolishness**
- **Cowardice**
- **Injustice**
- **Intemperance**

The Four Virtues are a useful way to summarise what the Stoics were trying to teach, and serve as a handy method of modelling ourselves, our opinions and our actions to begin our own path to eudaimonia. But what, you might ask, is eudaimonia?

IN SUMMARY

The Virtues are your guide to good actions.

Let Wisdom, Courage, Moderation and Justice be the foundations you build on.

We are what we repeatedly do. Excellence, then, is not an act, but a habit.

———

ARISTOTLE

CHAPTER 3

The Joy of Happiness

or All Is Equal

We all want to be happy. We spend most of our life chasing it, in one form or another – one more go on the bouncy castle, one more beer, one more evening scrolling on our phones. More than money, more than things, we want to have *happiness*. Isn't that why this book exists?

The Stoics believed there was a path to happiness, something clearly defined and simple to follow (not necessarily easy, but simple). They believed in seeking *eudaimonia*, best translated as 'human flourishing'. Happiness wasn't a state achieved by looking after yourself and fulfilling as many of your desires as possible – instead, it was achieved by living within this triangle of actions:

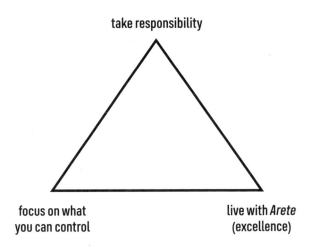

take responsibility

focus on what
you can control

live with *Arete*
(excellence)

By keeping within these three points, Stoics understood you could find harmony with your inner self, and with the world around you, and would find your happiness growing each day.

Let's look at those three actions:

1. Take responsibility

We all have hardships in our lives, of bigger and smaller sizes. But it's taking responsibility for the steps we choose afterwards that starts us on the path to eudaimonia. Do we let go of regrets and recriminations? Do we take physical and mental care of ourselves as and when needed? Do we engage with the world in a way that takes responsibility for what we can and can't control? Which leads us to . . .

2. Focus on what you can control

We'll look in the next chapter at the control we have over the world. We have little to no control over when we are born, when we die, certain illnesses or accidents, incidents of good or bad luck, our pasts, major global events and natural disasters, and what other people decide to do, among many, many other things.

All we have control over is our opinions, actions, choices and motivations, and our own character. So, while it may feel limiting to have so little control over something as large and important as our entire lives, it's also freeing to know this limited list is something we are able to manage and focus on.

3. Live with Arete

Arete often translates as 'excellence' or 'goodness', more specifically in this context the excellence that comes when following the Four Virtues – Wisdom, Justice, Courage and Moderation. By following these Virtues, the Stoics believed that you would naturally be putting yourself on the path to eudaimonia, because by encouraging Wisdom, Justice, Courage and Moderation in your life (and in the lives of those around you), you would discover the inner peace and happiness that comes with natural human flourishing.

There is a classical parable about Heracles, the great Greek hero, coming to a crossroads. There, he is invited by two goddesses to make a choice between their two paths. The goddess of vice, Kakia, promises him an easy, pleasant life, while the goddess of virtue, Arete, offers a difficult but glorious life. Of course, Heracles, like any good Greek, chooses Arete and suffers a most laborious struggle before achieving the status of a demi-god. But it does tell us that even two thousand years ago, philosophers grasped that easy wasn't generally better.

The sustainability and Stoicism researcher Kai Whiting believes that, as a Stoic, we have the duty to work towards the ideal of human flourishing. While similar to the Buddhist aspiration of Nirvana, which is frequently seen as freedom from the cycle of rebirth or a spiritual liberation, Nirvana is a goal to be (or not be) attained after maybe many lifetimes of striving. But eudaimonia is a path to be accessed immediately. Not after many lifetimes, but *now*.

Stoic eudaimonia starts the moment you step into that triangle. You don't have to have perfected the Four Virtues – you don't even have to have perfected acceptance over what can and can't be controlled; you don't yet have to have taken responsibility for every aspect of your life. But just deciding to start following the ideas of eudaimonia is enough to get you going. I compare it to a beautiful beam of golden light: it's not miles away, it's not lifetimes of learning. You can step into it right now and get stronger just by being in it. And the more you stay in that beam of light, the better you'll be at working towards the three actions.

The pleasure you gain from the pursuit of your desires can only exist when the object of desire is present, and even in the presence of your desire, the pleasure may dwindle and so the desire grows. We cannot rely on externals for happiness, because if the external is gone then so is the pleasure it provided us. But when we rely on things that are our own, such as wisdom, reason, integrity and the love of truth; by nature these things cannot be stolen from us. They are ours. It is not wise to rely on anything that can be given or taken from us.

Marcus Aurelius, as well as being the author of the *Meditations*, was an emperor of the Roman Empire.

He had enormous wealth and power and little need to restrain himself in anything, but thanks to his study of Stoicism, he recognised he was in no greater position than his forerunner in philosophy, Epictetus, who was born into slavery years before. According to Stoic principles, Epictetus in fact had greater access to eudaimonia because he had less wealth. The philosophers recognised that fame and fortune can actually hinder our path there because of the temptations of overindulgence, greed and excess. How much more easily could Marcus Aurelius stray from Moderation and Justice with all the gold, wine, jewels and power he could ever imagine? But character is about the things you do control – not your looks, your family, your gold, wine and power, not your follower numbers or likes. These are superficial things that are really about luck, more than anything, but your character is something you spend every single day working on and trying to improve, so a good character is truly admirable because it has come about *solely* because of your own choices and actions.

I think it frees us to really accept this idea at a deep level. Seeing millionaires and billionaires in private jets, huge homes, sleek cars and on constant tropical holidays can be crushing. How can we ever compete? Really, of course, we can't compete – we don't need to. In reality, as ridiculous as it sounds, we should feel sorry for them. They are having a great time, but they are a million miles away from living a good life. Their days may be filled with wealth and comfort, but what gap in their lives are they trying to fill with all this excess? What rich person ever said that day after day of uncontrolled luxury made them ultimately feel happier, more fulfilled and more at peace? Whether it's about the extreme gap between their income and that of the vast majority of the population, or what activity they're actually doing to get the money, it doesn't feel hugely ethical.

The 'likes' and attention they gain from living and publicising their deluxe days are so fleeting, and will only breed more hunger for them – more attention, more luxury, more exclusivity. The fulfilment of desires just leaves them empty, because all their efforts leave them with nothing that nourishes their mind or their spirit. Pleasure is not the same as happiness – pleasure is by its nature something that passes quickly, and the search for it is hollow because pleasure is hollow, only making us feel better for a short moment. It's a rollercoaster, offering great highs but then crushing lows when all we can think about is the next high, whether it's the super-wealthy looking for an even bigger super-yacht or an everyday worker living for the excess of the weekend nights out. Pleasure offers no consistency, only an endless race to catch up with something that doesn't truly exist.

Meanwhile, we can face financial hardships that the super-rich may not even be able to conceive of, but the flip side is that we have greater clarity and fewer distractions from that triangle of eudaimonia. Internal peace is the only thing that will bring consistent happiness.

I became aware of Master Shi Heng Yi a few years ago, after his TED Talk on self-discovery. He grew up in Germany, with Vietnamese parents, and had gone on to Kung Fu and Qi Gong at the Shaolin Temple. After completing several university degrees, Shi wanted to continue with the Shaolin discipline and founded the Shaolin Temple Europe at Otterberg, in Germany. I'd got in touch with him, with the idea that we might speak together for a film that our company could share.

When I visited the Shaolin Temple in Germany, Master Shi Heng Yi sat and talked with me for hours, speaking fluently and at length about many different ideas around mental development, spiritual growth and uniting body and mind. Although he said he'd never heard of Stoicism, he recognised that many Shaolin ideas and Stoic ideas echoed one another. In our conversation, he explained to me that despite his robes, his eloquent speech and the fact that others would consider him at the very top of the hierarchy within the Temple, at bedtime he takes everything off and showers just like any other person. Behind the presentation we allow the world to see, we are all simply our character, completely equal within. Later, he took us to the Shrine Room in the Temple, a beautiful space decorated with candles and a large golden Buddha statue. We watched as everyone lined up before the statue and bowed to it, putting their face to the floor and reciting their mantra. Afterwards, Master Shi Heng Yi said to me, 'The Buddha is just plastic. The exercise is to remind us to be humble, that none of us are too special to bow to a piece of plastic, no matter our position in society or in the Temple.' Even in that Temple, in the Shrine Room, with the Shaolin Master, all of us were equal. I could not imagine finding that same peace and consideration in the life of someone dedicated to accumulating power and wealth. In fact, the highest rates of depression, anxiety and self-harm in all its forms appear in the wealthiest countries. The psychiatrist and opioid addiction specialist Anna Lembke has spoken about how the richest nations in the world have 'overloaded our brains' reward pathways with too much dopamine', meaning that our lack of struggle to find good things – whether that's a tree full of fruit, a colourful distraction, a new stimulation – means that we constantly adjust our brain's 'normal' ever upwards. On a very real, neurological level, the more we have, the harder we find it to be happy with what we have because our brains adjust to that level of comfort and never shift 'down' with any of the normal, evolutionary difficulties of achieving fresh fruit, distraction or stimulation. This constant, easy access to a high-potency reward means that 'we're all unhappier, more anxious, more depressed, more irritable, less able to take joy in the things that used to give us joy or have given people joy for generations, and also [made us] more susceptible to pain.' Our modern technology has moulded our brains so it's scientifically harder for us to be happy when we use it.

When my brothers and I first started trying to build our business, that office in our mum's attic was so basic and our hours were long. We had such clear dreams about what we wanted: to buy our own studio, complete with filming and editing spaces. We worked so hard and eventually had enough luck to be able to buy the studio. We then spent a long time making it exactly how we wanted, complete with basketball courts. It was literally a dream come true. I spent a day enjoying it all, but then experienced a crushing sense of 'Oh . . .' After all that work, getting what we wanted wasn't, in fact, the answer to everything.

The more you desire, the more you admit to yourself that what you have right now is not enough. If you get into the habit of this mindset then even when you get what you desire, it won't be enough for you. On that day, I knew exactly what this meant. I had held that studio up to be everything I needed to be truly happy, and I would *not* be happy until I had it. Unfortunately, I wouldn't be happy when I had it, either, because 'getting' is very rarely the solution, no matter what we get. We had achieved the goal but lost the hope we had that this 'thing' would solve everything. And it didn't, because nothing can solve *everything*.

EXERCISE

Thinking about the Four Virtues, how much do you think you follow them in your daily life?

— Can you increase your own Wisdom, or your respect for it in others?

— Can you improve your daily actions towards fairness and your support of Justice in the world?

— Can you build up your Courage, whether at work, in relationships, towards your own goals or in support of a stranger?

— Can you look at Moderating your life — enjoying things but not too much, trying new things but maintaining a sense of stability?

Do you feel a shift in your life if you bear these things in mind every day for a week? Do you think your path is tending towards eudaimonia?

Well-being is realised by small steps
but is truly no small thing.
— ZENO

But what's the point of all this if I never achieve perfect eudaimonia? The difference between this and many other paths of enlightenment is that this is not necessarily a finishing point that we as Stoics aim for. It's a triangle that we can stand in – maybe we're closer to the edges, maybe we're just in one corner or maybe we've really studied Stoicism or we naturally tend towards these philosophies, and we're heading towards the centre of the triangle. We will slip up, we'll make judgements, we'll be greedy occasionally and be unfair on a bad day, but none of that means we've undone previous good work. We don't have to put off starting because we haven't yet nailed being perfect. It's a practice, a habit we develop every single day by engaging with Stoic principles and using the Four Virtues as tools to encourage our own positive routines, rather than an object to 'achieve'.

And the great thing about Stoicism is that it doesn't just benefit us, as philosophers. It benefits everyone. By focusing on eudaimonia, it is a flourishing of all humans; it's not self-care, but universal care, encouraging connection, education, empathy and generosity.

I'm frequently online working hard to spread the Stoic message, but as anyone who's online can tell you, your presence there means that you get negative messages you'd otherwise be able to avoid. At times I get daily hate messages, public notes or toxic DMs about my work and me personally. In the past, I would have been knocked down for weeks by the anger and criticism in them; now, I use Virtue Ethics – the guidance of the Four Virtues to shape my actions – to engage with the senders, to try to understand and support them. If I believe they've got a moral blindness in this particular area – that they think it's OK to message someone and talk to them in this way – part of my Stoicism means a responsibility to engage and help them.

It's not always easy, but when I'm struggling I treat it like a game, to twist their message into something positive, to interact with them with kindness in a way that will make them feel better. What's truly surprising is not how much better this method makes me feel, which it does, but how many of them come back with an apology, an explanation of their behaviour and an acceptance of the Stoic principle I've used in my own message. When I get those replies, it makes me happy to keep going. Now I feel that the worse the message is, the more excited I am by the challenge. Are they saying something true? Can I help them feel better? Something that was once horrible for me is now enjoyable.

You know from experience that in all your wanderings you have nowhere found the good life – not in logic, not in wealth, not in glory, not in indulgence: nowhere. Where then is it to be found? In doing what man's nature requires. And how is he to do this? By having principles to govern his impulses

and actions. What are these principles? Those of good and evil – the belief that nothing is good for a human being which does not make him just, self-controlled, brave and free: and nothing evil which does not make him the opposite of these.
— MARCUS AURELIUS

We are remarkable creatures and often don't realise how resourceful, strong and full of potential we are. According to Stoicism, everything we need mentally, emotionally and spiritually is within us.

We actually want what is good for us; while we might have cravings or addictions to sugar, drugs, alcohol or anything which in excess is bad for us, our minds are constantly seeking a middle path that follows the Four Virtues, and almost all of us naturally feel at our best when we are trying to be fair, moderate, brave and wise. There are constant external pressures and distractions that try to pull us away from eudaimonia, but that is the choice we are free to make: a path of positivity, where our practice makes our life and the lives of those around us better, where we live in the present and enjoy each moment, or a path of vice – foolishness, injustice, cowardice and intemperance.

The Stoics understood that there is good – the Four Virtues – and bad – the Four Vices – and everything else is simply an Indifference, there to be wielded in a way that matches either the Vices or the Virtues. So, wealth in and of itself is not bad, but how did you get it? How do you maintain or build upon it? How do you use that wealth? Similarly, good health is not necessarily 'good' – what about the good health of a terrible dictator? Or a strong body of an elderly relative in terrible mental decline, who wishes to no longer live through their deterioration? We can never have too much Wisdom, Courage, Justice and Moderation; by their very definition, they are positives for all. And if we work daily in the eudaimonia triangle, it means that habit shapes us more and more towards those Virtues, so that if everything was taken from us – our money, our name, our jobs, families, homes – we would still have those habits, and the freedom to choose a path of Arete. So, all those different aspects of our life, the indifferent facts that are there to be shaped into something good or bad: we can decide exactly how we use them.

Eudaimonia means every day is a path to positivity, not a race to an end goal, a path that encourages better life practices and more happiness. Isn't that what we all want, really?

EXERCISE

Remembering Heracles at the crossroads, how can you choose the path of Arete?

Let's take the example of using your phone. If you halved your phone time – or more – how different could your life look in a day, a week, a year?

If you could, right now, see two versions of yourself as you might look in ten years' time – the one who had taken the road of pleasure

---

and the one who had taken the road towards eudaimonia – do you think you could instantly tell the difference between them? What do you think those differences would be?

After just one day of making choices towards Arete, how different do you feel?

IN SUMMARY

All of us are equal in the eyes of Stoicism.

Live within the triangle of the three points: responsibility, what we can control, and pursuit of the Four Virtues.

Explore the path that encourages our own flourishing, and that of others.

CHAPTER 4

I Literally Can't Do Anything

or The Stoic View on a Chaotic World

It's easy to believe that the world is chaos. News happens faster than it can be reported, major events can seem out of control, and 24/7 internet and social media can make us feel like we will never be on top of everything we could, or should, be. Our brains are running at top speed, taking in more images and words daily than we might have previously seen in a week or even a month. We can have social connections with people all over the world who we've never met in real life, and family nearby who we only ever communicate with through a screen-chat.

But even two thousand years ago, Stoic philosophers understood that chaos is just a human perception. It's how we can choose – or not choose – to engage with everything around us. As a Stoic, you might be encouraged by *Amor Fati* – the Latin phrase that translates roughly as 'love of fate', the idea that we can't change what happens to us so we may as well make the best of it. This core principle of Stoic philosophy proposes that the world will happen how it happens, and almost none of it can be controlled by our choices.

Here are some things we can control:
— Our opinions and preferences
— Our actions and choices
— Our wants and motivations
— Our own character.

Here are the things we can't control:
— Things that have happened in the past
— Things that have been done by other people
— Natural disasters and accidents
— The decisions of others
— All other external events, situations and occasions.

At first glance, this may seem frightening or disheartening. But the more you think about it, the more comforting it is. Mark Twain, the great American writer, once said, 'I've had a lot of worries in my life, most of which never happened.' How many times have you worried about something and, in the end, it was either as bad as you feared or not as bad as you feared? Did worrying about it lessen any of your suffering? Or did you make yourself suffer twice as much by worrying about something out of your control? By understanding all the things you don't control, you free yourself up to expend your energy on the things you can.

Here are three ways of looking at the same Amor Fati philosophy:

You have power over your mind – not outside events. Realise this, and you will find strength.
— MARCUS AURELIUS

**Not being able to govern events, I govern myself,
and if they will not adapt to me, I adapt to them.**
— MICHEL DE MONTAIGNE

**Man is not worried by real problems so much as by
his imagined anxieties about real problems.**
— EPICTETUS

EXERCISE

Make a list of any events that you have worried about recently.

_____

_____

_____

_____

_____

_____

_____

> Did your worry help or harm you? If you accept that events will happen how the universe dictates, how much power does that give to your mind and your feelings?

In Stoicism, we talk about the idea of *sympatheia*, the belief that all of us are tied together by our natures and our existence and that we exist as a larger, single whole. However you choose to see this – fate, God's plan, Zeus's will, or through any other philosophical or religious framework – at its heart, the simple core idea is that to accept our lives as they truly are is to live at peace. Although in Stoicism we may make reference to gods, or God, or fate, you may have no belief in any of these. But it doesn't change the fact that we may wake up tomorrow and it's cold and rainy; whether you believe a god made the rain, or a complex series of weather patterns across the globe, the fact is that it's raining. It's been handed to you, and the only thing you can do about it is to accept what you're given and understand that things happen exactly and only as they happen.

There is a phrase commonly attributed to Zeno that says, 'When a dog is tied to a cart, if it wants to follow, it is pulled and follows, making its spontaneous act coincide with necessity. But if the dog does not follow, it will be compelled in any case. So it is with men too: even if they don't want to, they will be compelled to follow what is destined.'

So, how will we decide to behave today? Is this the day we stop being compelled and start walking? Since we have no way of stopping or even slowing the cart, no matter how difficult it may be to admit it, how does it change our lives to walk with the cart instead? Chrysippus, the third leader of the Stoic school, compared our potential fated lives to being either a cylinder or a cone. If we practise Stoicism and pursue the Four Virtues, we can become cylinders, going smoothly where life takes us and experiencing new things. Otherwise, we are like cones, pushed by the gods or by fate, but only ever circling the same ground, experiencing nothing new, feeling no progress, wondering why nothing seems to truly change.

If we accept that we have very little control over the world, we can, with practice, be thankful that the world has been predetermined and we can focus on the small control we really do have. Events are a passing moment, but the control we can practise over our character and our choices is the work of a virtuous life. Zeno, when his ship was wrecked and his lifetime's wealth was gone in an instant, didn't invent Amor Fati. It is a simple aspect of humanity that we can choose to develop in ourselves, a practical choice we have to discover to encourage the simple ideas of Stoicism that will improve our lives in multiple ways.

The world doesn't have to happen to us but can happen for us, for our development and growth. It throws everything at us, not waiting for us to be ready, just happening on and on every day. But if you start to think of life as material – nails and wood, bricks and screws – you can make a conscious choice to either flinch at these things coming at you as you get battered and bruised, or to pick up those materials and build yourself a life from them. If you choose to walk away from those materials, you won't just have missed out on being able to build something new, but those things will be active obstacles on your path, that will trip you up and injure you despite your efforts to ignore or run away from them.

Anxiety is real – I know, I've suffered from it and received treatment for it in the past. But it's also up to us how much time and space we give to it. When I choose to concentrate on the things within my power, I find that I worry so much less and give my brain the breathing space it needs to make better, clearer thoughts. I no longer act through fear or panic; instead, I let go of the illusion of control and give myself more control over the things that really matter – my thoughts, my feelings and my actions. As author Kamal Ravikant has observed, 'Most of our pain, most of our suffering comes from resistance to what is. Life is. And when we resist what life is, we suffer. When you can say yes to life, surrender to life and say: "Okay, what should I be now?" That's where power comes from.' If we can accept what actually is and stop our resistance to the truth – that is the real battle, the inner battle, not a battle with the world, because the world continues regardless of our feelings towards it. It's purely inside us, fighting the world that will happen anyway, with our ego, our stories and our biases.

Day to day, most of us might experience mental turbulence from events and behaviours that may seem small to someone not experiencing them, but when they are in our own life, they can add up to a sense of life being unpleasant, upsetting or even unliveable. People on our commute with noisy music, strong-smelling food or loud conversation. People at the gym leaving towels everywhere or hogging the machines. People in the street walking too slowly or pulling luggage on a crowded pavement; taking too long to find their card when it comes to pay or getting to the counter and not knowing what they want to order. It's stressful just thinking about it.

As with so much, the Stoics had thought about this. In the *Enchiridion*, a handbook of Stoic advice compiled by one of his students, Epictetus said, 'If you intend to engage in any activity, remind yourself what the nature of the activity is. If you are going to bathe, imagine yourself what happens in baths: the splashing of water, the crowding, the scolding, the stealing.' Even in second-century Greece, public spaces were filled with people exhibiting behaviours that annoyed others, because, if nothing else, people are always people, and we will always be bothered by one another's habits. But can we find a way to not be annoyed? How different do our days feel if we leave our beds each morning aware of the ways humanity bothers us?

It's not about ignoring habits we don't like, or behaving in a worse way because all behaviours should be acceptable as part of human nature. Instead, if we mentally prepare each day with an acceptance that these things happen; they have always happened; they always will happen, and our anger about them does nothing but leave us feeling angry; how differently can we experience each moment of our day. It is the disturbance to our sense of self and of 'rightness' that is upsetting at these times: this is not how we would do things, nor how we think it's right to do them. But if we go into a café already prepared to experience loud talkers, slow orderers and wallet-fumblers, those external actions will suddenly no longer bother us.

I talked about these ideas too with Master Shi Heng Yi at the Shaolin Temple Europe, discussing how disturbing it can be when strangers don't behave in the way your morals and beliefs dictate as 'right'. He asked me, 'The closest person to you in your life – are they capable of surprising you with their actions sometimes?' I thought about it and agreed, from time to time my partner would still surprise me. 'And the people next closest to you – do they surprise you too, with what they might do or say?' I agreed again, those family members or friends that I had known for years did still do things I wouldn't expect in the moment. The Master looked at me and asked, 'So why would you be so surprised by the behaviours of total strangers, those who you do not know or understand?' It was a viewpoint I had never experienced before. Of course, the world will be full of upsetting and bothersome stresses if we expect only to meet the experiences that match up with the experience of living inside our own heads, with our own choices, preferences and habits.

In the *Meditations*, Marcus Aurelius says, 'It would be absurd to be surprised at a fig-tree bearing figs. Remember that there is as little cause for surprise if the world brings forth fruits such as these when the crop is there.' We shouldn't be so upset at the world yielding the same fruit it always has; these behaviours aren't new, but we react as if we could never have guessed we'd find these things every time we left the house.

Our own internal world can seem like the 'right' way of doing things. But, of course, it isn't right – just right for us, for now. If we can accept this and understand that every living person has the same conflict between the internal 'correct' way the world should be and the reality of millions of people making different choices, that conflict disappears. The friction is no longer there, because our focus has shifted from being bothered by that difference, and instead moves to keeping our own character in a world full of external pressures. We can't choose how other people behave, only how we react to it.

Seek not for events to happen as you wish but rather wish for events to happen as they do and your life will go smoothly.
— EPICTETUS

There is a famous Chinese fable about a farmer and his horse. The farmer and his family lived close to the border of warring territories, and they relied on their horse to do the heavy work on the farm. One day, the horse ran away and the neighbours gathered to offer their condolences, knowing what a great loss it would be to the farmer. But he only said, 'Well, we don't know if this isn't for the better.'

A short while later, the horse returned and following it was a wild mare who wouldn't leave the horse's side. The neighbours gathered again to congratulate him on his great luck. But the farmer said, 'Well, we don't know if this isn't for the worse.'

The farmer's son loved to ride and would take the wild mare out daily. One morning, the son fell from the horse, broke his leg and was unable to walk for a long time. The neighbours visited once more, commiserating with the father for this terrible event. But the farmer replied, 'Well, we don't know if this isn't for the better.'

A short while later, war broke out at the border. All the young men in the area were conscripted to fight and hundreds were killed in the battles. But the farmer's son was left behind and spared because of his broken leg.

*

The farmer understood: nothing is objectively good or bad. We must accept what happens and not grieve or celebrate too hard for any event, because we do not know where the universe will take us next. Gifts may not always be a good thing; problems may not be as bad. Acceptance is the only way to deal with all that happens to us each day.

EXERCISE

A View from Above

Sit in a comfortable space and close your eyes. In your head, visualise yourself in your room. Then visualise your house or flat, then zoom out again to the whole street. Keep zooming out: your area, your country, your continent, up and up, Earth, the solar system, as far out into the universe as you can.

Let yourself dwell for a moment on how insignificant you are, a tiny, tiny speck in the universe. The vast majority of the universe will never know any of us lived or died – how many of your problems are something other than just temporary blips or complaints? Can you develop a new sense of perspective on the things that are troubling you?

When my brothers and I first started our business, working in our mum's attic with no guarantee of success and not even a salary coming in, we'd have constant migraines and stress headaches. In this busy household of seven siblings, the hours and pressure made us sick, the task always seemed impossible and sometimes it felt like too much. But I'd take five minutes out of my day to sit down in a quiet corner and do this exercise, and it would always put our struggles into perspective. What felt like impossible tasks were actually just steps along our chosen path, and we were lucky to be on it.

But what about when we are on our path, but not getting where we want to go? Perhaps we've worked really hard, but haven't got the home we wanted, or the holiday, or the small thing that will make us happy if we can just get it. Diogenes was a famous Cynic philosopher, a precursor to Stoic ideas, and was famous for living naked in a large wine-jar in the marketplace and using his simple life to criticise what he saw as a corrupt society. His sole possession was a wooden bowl, which he destroyed when he saw a boy drink instead from his cupped hands, exclaiming, 'Fool that I am, to have been carrying superfluous baggage all this time!' One story tells that Alexander the Great, creator of one of the largest empires in history, visited Diogenes. Alexander was delighted to meet such an acclaimed philosopher and asked him what favour he could grant the penniless man. Diogenes replied, 'Yes, move out of the sunlight.' Alexander then told him, 'If I wasn't Alexander, I should wish to be Diogenes.' So Diogenes replied, 'If I was not Diogenes, I would also wish to be Diogenes.' He recognised that Alexander, the richest man in the world and commander of thousands, still had desires driving him and despite all his possessions and power, he would always be falling behind in his achievements, never content with what the universe had given him. But Diogenes, naked in a wine-jar and drinking from his hands, wanted only to nap in the sunlight. He had everything he could possibly desire.

More than that: who are we to know what is right for us at any given time? The Dalai Lama said, 'Remember, sometimes not getting what you want is a wonderful stroke of luck.' Like the farmer in the fable, we don't know what is good or bad for us, what disaster may lead to something wonderful, and what good fortune may be a curse. And if events don't develop into something unexpected, perhaps any hardship is exactly what will lead us to develop and strengthen as a person. Albert Camus said, 'In the midst of winter, I found there was, within me, an invincible summer,' and Fyodor Dostoevsky wrote, 'The darker the night, the brighter the stars.' Two thousand years ago, the philosopher Seneca recognised the importance of hardships to an improved life, writing, 'No man is more unhappy than he who never faces adversity. For he is not permitted to prove himself.' Life's blessings and sufferings should be treated the same: as impermanent states that we travel through to polish our character and improve ourselves. Missing out on something we wanted could, with the right outlook, be the best thing that ever happened to us (if you're going through difficulty right now, remember this).

So, a Stoic mindset is one where we embrace an attitude that makes the best out of anything that happens and all that we have. If external control is an illusion, we must embrace the moment we are in to make the best of it. The past has already happened and cannot be changed, and the future is not happening currently so cannot be changed either. We can spend hours each day worrying about both of these things – the mistakes we made, the regrets we have, the choices we could have made differently; the difficulties we might face, the losses we might suffer, the humiliations we might experience – but none of those things are 'real'. Regret is just our way of dragging a past mistake into our future, and fear is a pain we imagine that we need to feel.

The past and future cannot be affected by the things we control, our own actions right now, so we can accept them and live according to the principles of Stoicism or we can continue to suffer for things that have no tangible truth in reality.

The whole future lies in uncertainty: live immediately.
— SENECA

Memories can be shaped. How often has a new understanding or discovery made you look at a memory differently? Something sweet became bitter with this new knowledge or an unpleasant memory took on a softer lens when we understood more about a situation? But the event didn't change, only our feelings towards it. So why would we accept that we should constantly be held hostage by memories, making us suffer for things that are past, unchangeable and objectively beyond our control? Why not instead learn to accept the feelings as just that, *feelings*, and not that our pain is a truth about the universe to carry until the day we die?

Our future, too, can seem overwhelming. Our jobs, our friends and family, our hopes and plans, not to mention conflict and difficulties in the news every day: how much do each of those things weigh on our mind? Can we live a 'good' life if we are being crushed by fears and anxieties about the future? Why not recognise that these anxieties too are not 'real'? Events may happen; they may not. Little that we do will change much of where the world will go. We can be controlled by our thoughts or we can accept the Stoic view of Amor Fati and focus instead on the single moment we are living in.

Now, this might seem impossible. How can you just ignore huge issues like war or climate change? The answer, of course, is that it is not about ignoring them, but about what you can do in this moment. People in terrible situations across the world and throughout history still show extraordinary humanity and kindness to others.

Grief can be a powerful reminder of how much we have loved and been shaped by our love for someone – after all, would you want your loved ones to remember you with overwhelming grief for the rest of their lives, or to gradually be able to celebrate and feel joy that they had known you? We can live in a moment of suffering and still connect with the very best life can offer us.

So, how do we move from acceptance to joy and fully embrace Amor Fati?

There are three key aspects:
— To welcome challenges and difficulties as opportunities for growth and development.
— To let go of regrets about the past and focus on making the most of our present moment.
— To practise and cultivate a sense of appreciation for the experiences that come our way.

None of these might come easily to begin with. As the seventeenth-century Chinese strategist and philosopher Miyamoto Musashi said, 'It may seem difficult at first, but all things are difficult at first.' But practising these three aspects daily will gradually become easier. Failure is not a reason to give up, it is a part of learning a new way of living. The more we practise, the more this way of thinking becomes a habit – we start to view the whole world differently when we get into a habit of gratitude, acceptance and opportunity.

IN SUMMARY
You know that rude people exist, so you don't have to be surprised or troubled by them.
Accept the universe the way it is, and your life will run smoothly.

Some things are within our power, while others are not. Within our power are opinion, motivation, desire, aversion, and, in a word, whatever is of our own doing; not within our power are our body, our property, reputation, office, and, in a word, whatever is not of our own doing.

———

EPICTETUS

CHAPTER 5

If It Ain't Broke, You Can't Fix It

or Control and Out of Control

One of the joys of Stoicism is the way that all the principles fit together, all feeding each other and meshing perfectly. But having said that, the concept of control – or rather, lack of control – might be at the very heart of Stoicism. In fact, it's absolutely key to fitting all those other ideas around it.

The Dichotomy of Control is a simple idea: the understanding that there are things within our control – and things that are not. The more we try to gain control of our lives, the less control we have; the more we realise how little control we have, the less we struggle, the less we worry. We try to control our status and where we are in life but fail to recognise that our goals, plans and ambitions are just words and images in our head; they have no reality to them at all, they are just part of our internal narrative. They can feel like the most important things in our lives, but these words and images have no control over life at all; life just keeps on going, regardless of what we are picturing 'should happen'.

A criticism of the Dichotomy of Control is that if someone fails – if they try to take control of a situation beyond them – then Stoicism makes them feel bad, that they are somehow 'failing' at living life successfully. Of course, Stoic philosophy is far more forgiving than this: Stoics know that control does not mean mastery. We use our reason as best we can to influence our desires, opinions and control based on the Four Virtues, but we all recognise that just as reason is in the nature of humanity, so are mistakes. It's not about feeling a failure, but recognising life is a challenge to be accepted and enjoyed. The release of control – and the control over ourselves – is a lifelong lesson.

One of my quotes that's most shared online is, 'You can dance in the rain, or sulk in the rain, it will rain regardless.' People seem to instantly grasp that life is filled with choices, not control, and that only by accepting our chance to make positive choices will we regain any sense of peace over our lives. All we can control is our reaction to life.

It often seems like we have control over aspects of our lives, but that's just an illusion. For instance: if I want to improve my health, I can go to the gym, right? But going to the gym could also result in a serious injury and I'm slowed down for a long time. Perhaps I could eat much more healthily to help my body; but maybe it'll cost me much more money. So, I could earn more money by working harder and getting a different job, that's within my control, isn't it? Yes, but you don't know if working harder, or in a new job, might result in so much stress that you can't work at all, and mean you're in a harder financial situation. What about building up your reputation? You can do all kinds of things to build up your reputation online or in your local area, but at what cost? What if your efforts result in someone becoming jealous and deciding to talk badly about you? You can't control it, but now your reputation is worse than when you began.

*

It's not about looking at the most negative possible option. It is about recognising that these feelings of 'control' aren't real, but are illusions founded only on things external to us. There are so many variables in every single step up and step down that might happen to you in your lifetime, that there is no point in investing in the idea that you control your life. Illness, accidents, other people's actions are completely out of our control, and will happen no matter what we do.

Stoicism isn't about having an iron grip on your existence. Stoicism means remembering Amor Fati and the few things we can control:
— Our opinions and preferences
— Our actions and choices
— Our wants and motivations
— Our own character.

It's not much, is it?

EXERCISE

You might be feeling stressed or worried about something in your life. Maybe it's something huge, a global event; maybe it's something just affecting you, like a work presentation or a trip out with friends.

Take a piece of paper and draw two columns. At the top of the left-hand column write 'Things I Can Control' and at the top of the right-hand column, 'Things I Can't Control'. Just thinking about the one thing that's on your mind, fill out the columns as realistically as you can (don't try to take responsibility for things beyond your reach).

How much longer is the list of things you can't control? How much more manageable does the list of things you can control seem?

Now you're free to just focus on that short list of things you can, realistically, control.

Sometimes it's nice to feel swept away by 'things that don't really matter'. It can feel fun to scroll on our phones and read about the latest celebrity scandal or gossip about a TV personality. But before we know it, we have strong opinions about their stories and behaviour, feel genuine emotions in our bodies and minds for people we don't even know and are unlikely to meet or ever be directly affected by. Similarly, I'm baffled by people who are passionate about their sports team. People are made so ecstatic and so miserable by the actions of their team, feeling real anger for weeks at a time, but the fans' anger won't affect the play in any way whatsoever. Yet the fans allow their moods and their lives to be shaped by something far beyond their control.

We try to control everything, from the traffic and weather to other people's opinions of us, putting hours of energy and focus every day into things that will remain unaffected by our efforts. We give 99% of our life to these things, and to thoughts of the past and future, handing over our attention and drive to something completely external. Whatever we try to do about these things, the events will happen anyway, the past will have occurred, the future will happen when it does, and everything will go on regardless of our thoughts. It's like standing in the sea and trying to fight the waves back, and then wondering why we're exhausted and nothing is different.

The fact is those few things that we can control have one thing in common. They are all internal, within our minds and bodies. The second we accept that internal energy is all that matters, that our opinions, actions, motivations and character are the only things we have control over, is the moment that we actually gain control over our lives. That realisation is like a superpower – imagine suddenly being told you could have 99% more energy and focus, that you could grow and develop more swiftly as a person, with less to worry about, and carrying less mental weight. Wouldn't anyone want that?

Stoicism is like a cheat code for life. Instead of noise and busyness for the sake of it, running around in circles, we can just walk, pause and look around, breathe the air and listen to the sounds. Be bored! Give up control and enjoy all the freedom it gives you.

External things are not the problem. It's your assessment of them. Which you can erase right now.
— MARCUS AURELIUS

There's a tendency in our modern lives to want everything done now, to achieve achievement without appreciating the process that got us there. It's called 'destination addiction', the belief that we'll finally be happy when we reach that goal – it's in the future, but it's coming, and we just need to do X, Y and Z (or, more realistically, we just 'need' to do A, B, C . . . all the way to Z).

By seeking to fulfil our destination addiction, it means that we crave control even more – of our physical strength, our mental states, our status, even our physical processes of growing and ageing. How many times have we rushed back to work after only a day or two off with illness, when we know our bodies need time to heal fully and recover? How often do we buy products to rush something our body does perfectly well if we treat it with care and respect? Modern life is shaped for us to hurry and rush through it. So, how quickly can we grasp all the things we have no effect on?

It was a slow process for me to understand the Dichotomy of Control. Of course, I didn't want to give up *any* control – how could I possibly succeed if I stopped focusing so hard on everything? It seemed like a weakness to give up control, to let myself accept my life, to a great extent, was completely out of my hands.

It took practice. First, I tried to recognise whenever I was feeling frustrated, and just let the experience that was causing me frustration wash over me. If I was stuck in traffic, I wasn't running behind or being delayed – I was being given an opportunity to sit and watch the world. I remembered a story I'd heard about a group of people stuck at a level crossing for a long time while a super-extended train passed by. The adults were furious, but the child in the crowd turned to her mother and said with admiration and amazement, 'Wow! This train is so long!'

We have that same opportunity every day. Let's break it down to its most basic form:

Issue	Benefit
Stuck in traffic	Extra time to listen to music or watch the world
Rude people	A chance to practise compassion
Burnt the meal	Opportunity to try a new meal with leftover ingredients
Tickets all sold out	Can do something else you wouldn't otherwise have tried
Holiday cancelled	Engage with that To-Do list you've never got around to
Not picked for a team	More time to support the team with off-pitch needs

We can look back on the 'bad' times in our life and appreciate what we gained from them: a partner leaving us made us later find a better relationship and realise how damaging the current one was. My labouring boss was so awful and my wages so low that I didn't stay in that job and realised more of my potential. Even the death of a loved one can sometimes work to unite a family.

If we are stuck in traffic, we are stuck in traffic, and anger won't change that. Maybe we can listen to music, talk to someone else in the car or just notice life through the car window. If we have cleaning to do, the cleaning needs to be done, but rather than rushing through it to reach what we 'really want to do', it's a chance to do something thoughtfully, to do it to the best of our abilities, to listen to something good and take our time to make the cleaning a job well done. Recently, when I had some garden work to do, someone offered to help me with it so I'd finish sooner. But the job was to work on the garden, not to do it as fast as possible and throw that experience over my shoulder before rushing on to the next thing; the enjoyment came from doing the job, savouring the moments within it, not hurrying to have a completed task. I didn't want to develop destination addiction, I wanted to practise savouring what I did with my time. I appreciated the offer but finished it alone in the knowledge that I also appreciated every moment I'd been able to spend doing it. Do any of us want to look back on our lives and consider the hours, months, years we've 'lost' to chores and errands? Or would things feel different if we'd been able to respect each task as a task that needed doing – it wasn't robbing us of our time, our time was still there to be enjoyed as we completed the task and enjoyed it for what it was.

If we think of life as a line, with our birth at one end and our death at the other, there are all sorts of events happening all the way through, taking us in all kinds of directions:

Our birth is the first moment, and our death is the ultimate destination. So, what are we rushing for? All those squiggly lines in the middle are the ones we want to sit and really experience – they are all we can experience because everything else is out-side of our life. All that is waiting for us as we hurry through our time is the end of our existence, and we never know when it will come. Sometimes we have a good conversation with a friend, a talk worth remembering, the kind of conversation where you have tears running down your face and a painful belly from laughing so hard. I'm not sure of the meaning, but with a good talk to a friend I'm sure it is to be present, to laugh, to share the experience; it is to feel the moment for what it is. You do not meet up with a friend to finish the conversation as fast as possible. As for music, it is the highs and lows; the enjoyment of the beautiful symphony, a sound so captivating it speaks to your soul. There'd be no enjoyment in one quick note of a song; just as in life, the joy comes from the rises and falls, the developments and our reactions to each one as it comes after the one before.

The writer and 'philosophical entertainer' Alan Watts once said that life was like a dance, and that 'when you are dancing, you are not intent on getting somewhere'. It's about the journey, not the destination.

The Stoics see any event as having three parts:
— Awareness
— Assessment
— Action.

In any given event, I gain awareness of it, what's happening, and I take action, reacting to what's happened. But in between is assessment, the microscopic moment where we put our value judgements on and ask, 'How does this harm me?' With practice, Stoics believe we can change that question to 'How can I do what's best in this situation?' By building the habit, we can find the space to take control of our actions by extending our assessment time to as long as we need – maybe it's by counting to ten and making space in our anger to see things more objectively, or by developing a third-person perspective to understand that if we get drawn in to, say, an argument by our emotions, all we'll be is another emotional person arguing. We won't actually have made things any better for anyone.

If you've ever been in any kind of accident, you'll know that very often we become aware of something bad having happened, a knee-jerk assessment of how bad it could be, and a poorly thought-through reaction to what we imagine could have happened and who may be at fault. Instead, the Stoic approach is to get a clearer awareness of what has occurred; use that clarity to make a less panicked and more truthful assessment and react according to what we can control about the clearly assessed situation. Can you try that next time you experience an accident of some sort?

I face challenges every day, big and small, and the way I manage them now is by gamifying my life. Every time I face a difficulty, I tell myself that I've got the chance to level up by doing the right thing, and the reward I get each time I manage it is to build my character and to increase the good I've put into the world. I've got no control over the behaviour of others, their rudeness, their selfishness, someone in a bad mood, someone being aggressive. But the control I do have is over my own actions, and when you start building that muscle it gets stronger and stronger. It might seem overwhelming at first, but the idea of it being a game means that I just do it in bite-size chunks – this supermarket trip, this short drive, this single commute.

EXERCISE

Next time someone is mean to you, or rude, or behaves in a way that you don't like, pretend this is just a game – let's call it Stoicism™. The goal of Stoicism™ is to build your character, and the way you do it is to behave according to the Golden Actions of Stoicism™ (also known as the Four Virtues). So, you're in the game and someone pushes in front of you in a queue. What would a Stoic do? In the game, you know the best way to increase your points total is to look to the Four Virtues. Maybe that's not what you would normally do in real life, but this is Stoicism™!

Every time you leave the house, it's a potential Stoicism™ mission, and a chance to build those points.

Try this for a few days. Perhaps without your realising it, while you play you'll be levelling up your patience, perspective and empathy. How does it feel?

It is not daily increase but daily decrease, hack away the unessential. The closer to the source, the less wastage there is.
— BRUCE LEE

Bruce Lee was talking about both his martial arts training and his life – and this echoes precisely the Stoic principles we've been talking about. In the Dichotomy of Control, you hack away at all those things you really don't have control over and you are left with the essential: the true core of life, where you can practise following the Four Virtues to better your own life and the lives of those around you. Suddenly, life is not just manageable, but it's enjoyable.

Many of us feel like therapy could, or has, helped us to find life more manageable and enjoyable. CBT, or cognitive behavioural therapy, is an acclaimed form of talking therapy used by millions around the world, based around changing how you think and behave. It actually has Stoic roots. Perhaps you know the famous Serenity Prayer from 1934, written by theologian Reinhold Niebuhr:

> God, give me the serenity to accept the
> things I cannot change; the courage to change
> the things I can; and the wisdom to know
> the difference.

From these foundations and Modern Stoic beliefs, psychologist Albert Ellis founded Rational Emotive Behaviour Therapy (REBT), the first form of CBT, propounding the belief that our emotional difficulties aren't caused by events happening outside our bodies, but by our own personal and often irrational interpretations around the events. This echoes perfectly Epictetus's own quote, 'The chief task in life is simply this: to identify and separate matters so that

I can say clearly to myself which are externals not under my control, and which have to do with the choices I actually control.' Likewise, Marcus Aurelius wrote, 'Choose not to be harmed – and you won't feel harmed. Don't feel harmed – and you haven't been.' Taking the time to find space in what is really happening means that we don't have to focus on the harm that might have been caused to us, but instead on what we can do to get through the situation, and to grow from it – maybe even to help someone else. It's an opportunity to get involved and entangled with other people's existence, and a chance to show how Stoicism could improve lives beyond our own. CBT is a brilliant tool for a short-term treatment with Stoic principles, but Stoicism as a life philosophy can be beneficial for many more people, forever.

When you wake up in the morning, tell yourself:
the people I deal with today will be meddling,
ungrateful, arrogant, dishonest, jealous and surly.
They are like this because they can't tell good

from evil. But I have seen the beauty of good, and the ugliness of evil, and have recognised that the wrongdoer has a nature related to my own . . . We were born to work together like feet, hands and eyes, like the two rows of teeth, upper and lower.

— MARCUS AURELIUS

If we think back to the introduction to this book, to Zeno losing everything he owned in a shipwreck, we can see what a Stoic he was already. He didn't fret or weep at the disaster; instead, he went looking for answers. The ship was gone, the event had occurred – but now he had a chance to understand what humans needed to not just cope, but flourish when things like this happened.

As we looked at in Chapter 3, I get hate comments as long as I have an online presence, and I realised fairly soon that I had two options: to focus on them and the way they make me feel (pretty bad, to begin with) or to think about my response, using Stoicism to educate them about the Stoic philosophy. I have no control over their comments or the way they think about me, but I *can* choose to work alongside these commenters. I had comments recently about my hair and how bad it looked – in the past, this would have sent me into a tailspin and I would have been rushing off to the barber (if I dared leave the house to begin with). Now, I see this as an opportunity to teach someone the education they need. That's something I can choose.

Years ago, I was travelling across New Zealand with two friends in a cheap and terrible car. The gasket had blown and we had no money to fix it. What it meant in practicality was that we had to stop every five miles to find a lake, river or garage to pour in water to cool the engine, and my friends quickly got sick of it and just wanted to ditch the car. Instead, I put a dumb song on the car radio and we were all soon laughing, and that event became a happy memory for us all. We didn't have control over the condition of our transport, but we could make our own choice about how we'd deal with it and experience our trip. Soon after, we were lucky enough to meet a couple who drove us all the way to our destination – and would they have offered so easily if we'd been stressed and fighting over the blown gasket? Maybe not.

I'm not fully there yet, of course, because I'm just human. I take comfort though from the fact that I'm not alone – even Marcus Aurelius seemed to have struggles with the Stoic principles, which we can see in his *Meditations*. Written as a private journal, the *Meditations* are Marcus Aurelius's notes to himself, and we can read in his many notes about anger that he clearly suffered with managing his temper. And this was one of the greatest Stoic philosophers of all time! He didn't have much luck with his son, either – after Marcus Aurelius lived as one of the most successful, celebrated emperors of Rome, his cruel, corrupt son Commodus devalued the currency, created massacre-filled gladiatorial shows and brought an end to the golden age of the Roman Empire. In an age where it was tradition for emperors to choose their successors, Marcus Aurelius bet everything on his own son, giving him the finest teachers, the greatest military training, the best opportunities any young man in the Empire could possibly have. He believed that with all his own skills and wisdom, and the flesh and blood of his own son, he could create another great world leader – even on his deathbed, he said, 'Go to the rising sun; I am already setting.' He wanted all his advisers to focus on his son and the future he would build.

And yet Marcus Aurelius failed. Even he, with every resource at his fingertips and all his accumulated knowledge, could not succeed in making Commodus into the man he'd hoped for. It may be that Marcus Aurelius strived so hard to be a great man that his real struggle was to be a good man. Like the idea of isolation and domination being an illusion of strength, when the reality is that true strength requires connection and letting life exist within us – perhaps the path of Marcus Aurelius's life as leader of an empire meant that all his Stoicism led him to be the greatest of men in pursuit of eudaimonia, when really his goal should have been to be simply Good.

Perhaps his writings teach us so well because he knew how hard it could be. But we should be reassured by this – that even now his writings inspire so many, and the effects of his work are still bringing good into the world.

IN SUMMARY

Remember that most of our problems lie outside our control. Enjoy the release from feeling that you should be controlling things 'better'.

All you can do is focus on the internal control that you do have.

We are always complaining that our days are few, and acting as though there would be no end of them.

———

SENECA

CHAPTER 6

At Least You've Got One Certainty

or Death Is Inevitable

I t sounds a bit heavy, doesn't it? *Death is inevitable.* A bit gloomy for a philosophy that's promising to improve your life?

I used to be terrified of death when I was a young boy. For years, I'd keep myself up for hours at night, absolutely petrified at the thought of my own death. I was frightened to go to the shops, terrified to talk to people, frightened to approach anyone even if I wanted to help them. I was powerless, held hostage by my fears about what people might think of me, how I might die, how I might fail at living properly. I felt like I was barely living at all.

Then at school, a Religious Studies lesson was focusing heavily on what every religion thought came after death, whether that was heaven, paradise, rebirth or something else. I thought: what if all the religions have got it wrong? What if we die and that's it, no stress, no worries. It sounded to me – forgive the pun – like heaven. And if I was wrong, and there was a religion that had got it correct, then I'd end up in some kind of paradise eventually, or purgatory at worst. I could live with that thought. Why would religious followers find death so frightening if it would bring them closer to meeting their god or gods? Does that fear of death hold us back from living the best life we could? At home one night, I had another sudden realisation: when I died, I wouldn't know. My death would mean I was freed from any suffering or any consequence – my death would mean that my life, and all my experiences, good or bad, would be over. And that release meant that life was finite, and I didn't have forever to keep worrying about it. That night, I slept soundly, and never worried about death again: after all, I don't remember life before I was born, so I'm certain I won't remember life after I'm dead. (I heard a joke the other day that reminded me of my pre-Stoic mortality fears. 'Being dead is like being stupid; it only hurts the people around you.')

But maybe you don't worry about death, perhaps because you never think about it. In our Western culture, it isn't particularly normal to spend a lot of time thinking about death. It's seen as a bit odd, like we're inviting death in or dwelling on something a bit distasteful and weird. In fact, in ancient Rome, the feelings were the same: the Greeks and Romans didn't even like to say the name of Hades in case that conjured up their own mortality.

Which is, if you think about it, extremely odd. Of every single human who has ever lived or will ever live, from the richest to the poorest, the oldest to the youngest, in every country and with every possible life experience, only one thing binds us all: that every one of us will die. It's not up for debate, no one can buy their way past death with huge wealth, no one can cure it or run from it. It is a completely universal truth about life, that it ends for each of us, and everything around us, with death. (There's a famous story about the Zen master Ikkyu. Even as a boy he was bright and clever, so when he broke his master's precious antique teacup, the young Ikkyu hid the pieces of the cup behind him. When the master came in, Ikkyu asked, 'Why do people have to die?' The master replied with great patience, 'This is natural. Everything has to die and has just so long to live.' The boy held out the pieces of the broken cup and said, 'It was time for your cup to die.')

So, should we discuss death more? Or is it too upsetting? Should we be celebrating life instead of thinking about something as potentially frightening and bleak as death?

Stoic philosophers believed in *Memento Mori*, the remembrance of death. Two thousand years ago, citizens who followed the Stoics would carry coins with that phrase, or skulls and hourglasses, to remind them of the inevitability of the end. Even before that, the jar-dwelling Cynic philosopher Diogenes attempted to address his followers' queasiness at his certain death. When asked how he wished to be buried, he told them not to worry, that they could just toss his body outside the city walls for animals to feed on him.

Horrified at the idea, they begged him to reconsider. 'Fine,' he said. 'Just leave me with a stick to chase the animals away!' His followers hesitated, unsure exactly how to remind Diogenes that his stick-wielding days would be over, but he saw their confusion. If he no longer possessed the awareness to wield a stick, why should he care what happened to his physical remains? In the twenty-first century, my own equivalent of Diogenes's sense of mortality is a Memento Mori calendar, a single large poster with thousands of gridded squares, where I black out each day that passes to remind me how finite my life is.

My partner and I are also preparing a Death Box, as morbid as it might sound. We're filling it with our wishes for after we die, preferences for our funeral and things to leave for our daughter. It felt like a strange idea when my partner first suggested it, but I've grown to love the visceral sense of mortality it gives – I know people struggle even with the idea of a will, superstitiously believing that just writing one will cause them to need it, but this has really brought home our own Memento Mori, a physical sense of what will be left once we inevitably die, in one tiny box. What would you put in yours?

You could leave life right now. Let that determine what you do and say and think.
— MARCUS AURELIUS

As Marcus Aurelius said in his *Meditations*, 'No, you do not have thousands of years to live. Urgency is on you. While you live, while you can, become good.' Few people would choose to live forever. Maybe a little longer, maybe a lot longer, but not forever. Whatever length we put on life, there is an end to it, and it is that end that lends us urgency and purpose. And it isn't just life that ends, but all things. When I went out recently with my brothers, I was suddenly struck by the thought that I had no way of knowing if this was the final time we would all be together. If it wasn't this time, it would be another. And rather than feeling crushed by it, it made our time all the more precious because it was finite. There will always be a last time we hug a friend, cook a particular meal, watch the clouds and do our morning commute. Whether it's a good experience or a bad one, every occurrence has a final time.

So, how can we make that into a positive, every day?

I often think to myself that the most important thing I ever learned was the fact that I would die. Perhaps it wasn't learning this that changed my life, it was the acceptance of death that woke me up from the monotonous and the mindset of procrastination. It is odd to think that remembering my own mortality has brought me so much life, and remembering death daily makes the days more vibrant and real. Death is not the enemy; a wasted life is the enemy – for one is a guarantee and the other is a failure on our part. What could make life more precious than the awareness of it passing by? Death is *not* the enemy. Recognising and remembering death breathes new value into life – it's a precious gift that most of us don't even dare look at, let alone cherish.

EXERCISE

A man once said, 'I like to imagine I've already died, and I've begged God for just one more chance to walk in the woods, have my heart broken, be in love, do even the most mundane daily things. And I try to live as if God has granted me this one chance.'

Sit somewhere comfortable and safe, and close your eyes. Imagine you have only ten minutes to live – everything is about to be taken from you, every person, every opportunity, every potential experience. What regrets would you have in those ten minutes? What would you be wishing you could do again? Both bad and good, positive and negative – you could have one more chance at experiencing them all. Imagine the loss of it all, and imagine being given the chance to have them back again. Who would you like to talk to one more time?

After you've thought about your final wishes, ask yourself: how does that make you feel about the small things, like tasting something or drinking fresh water? And what about the bigger things, like seeing your friends and family again? How can you let those wishes shape today? How can you wake up each morning and live a life you won't regret?

One phrase often attached to Stoicism is that of *Carpe Diem* – to seize the day. If this day was your last, what would you do with it? Of course, few of us have the free time or the money to live like this constantly; whatever our passions, we simply aren't able to follow them at the expense of our responsibilities. But what about living with no regrets – if this day was your last, how would you like to conduct yourself? What sort of person do you hope to be remembered as? What tone would you like that final day to have?

Philosophers, writers, artists and poets have recognised throughout the ages that death is what gives life its value. If we had infinite time with everyone we loved, infinite opportunity to travel where we wanted, to read what we intended, to try every job we had an interest in, where would the urgency come from? How could we have any sense of focus or priority when we have infinite opportunity? It's the same as having a limitless supply of anything – we are unable to value or treat with respect that which seems to have no end. But when we're on our final teabag, how much more precious is that cup of tea? If we can only afford one meal out, how much more special does that meal seem than if we could go out every night, whenever we wanted?

Our lives are limited and, what's more, we have no way of knowing when the end will come.

Perfection of character is this: to live each day as if it were your last, without frenzy, without apathy, without pretence.
— MARCUS AURELIUS

As well as avoiding major regrets of action or behaviour on any potential deathbed, we can look at how we choose to spend each minute we have. Nowadays, it's all too easy to open our phones and suddenly, mindless swiping has taken hours out of our day. As the writer and philosopher Aristotle warned, 'the wasted life' is 'the saddest of all tragedies'. So, how can we avoid a wasted life?

It's not about never picking up your phone, or sitting on the sofa in the evening, or even just staring out of the window. But the Stoics encourage us to do all these things with purpose *and* mindfulness. We can build lives on bad foundations, on the basis of greed, fear, ego, consumption or anger. We can choose to spend our time online, looking at other people's lives and being envious of what they have, planning how to buy our own versions, worrying our lives don't look the same, or getting angry that other people don't treat us in the same way. What value do any of these actions have to your real, waking life? Imagine you lived in the middle of nowhere, no phone, no news, no social media. You wouldn't be aware of how angry you are supposed to be, you wouldn't be aware of what trend you should be keeping up with, you wouldn't have any knowledge of how scared you are suppose to be. Wouldn't you like to be – even occasionally – totally unaware? What is the mood you want your life to have?

Marcus Aurelius said, 'It is time to realise that you are a member of the universe, that you are born of Nature itself, and to know that a limit has been set to your time. Use every moment wisely, to perceive your inner brilliance, or it will be gone and nevermore within your reach.' Perhaps now is that time to decide what really matters to you, and what doesn't.

It's a simple habit to get into, thinking we'd all be happy if only for one small thing: an object we want, a job we should have, a person who ought to act the way we want. But if you get that one thing, will you truly be happy forever? Life is not about acquisition, but about experience. Death hangs over us to focus our minds on the experiences we are having, and only we can choose how to react to them. Do we spend our lives looking only for the most comfortable, pleasurable existence? As Marcus Aurelius said, 'Is a world without pain possible? Then don't ask the impossible.' And if a painless life is impossible, how do we deal with a reality that is filled with friction and difficulty?

EXERCISE

Open your phone and look at your screen time for the past seven days. Is it more or less than you expected?

If you multiply your daily hours by 365, and divide that number by 24, you'll get the number of days (without stopping for sleep) per year you are currently spending on your phone. (As a rough idea, two hours a day equates to a full month looking at your phone every year; six hours a day is three months of every year on your phone).

Write down what else you could have done with that time.

Can you aim to halve that time within a month? By using apps or taking up new habits and hobbies, can you turn your life from something you won't cherish, and may regret, at the end of your life into something that will build your character, boost your community or bring you face to face with other people?

By taking back some of those hours from your phone, is your mind able to relax and process more? Take note of whether your sleep and functional skills improve.

Boredom can often feel like a kind of death. How many times were you so bored as a child, or when you've been unable to access the internet, that you've said, 'I'm going to *die* if I can't find something good to do.' It feels like a waste of our life, like a punishment for something we didn't do or like something crushing about the state of reality will crash in on us when we're facing being bored.

Phones offer us the perfect frictionless escape from boredom. They are quick to access and open up a near-limitless world of distraction, entertainment and information. If you're stuck in a long queue or waiting for the next train, why wouldn't you swipe and tap into something much more interesting when the opportunity is there? But for the convenience and the time-killing that you gain, you lose far more of much greater value: the chance to engage with the real world, in a way only your living body can, and the chance to experience *boredom*.

Boredom is seen as the greatest possible waste of time, and of life, in our fast-paced Western capitalist culture. How can you be bored when you could be networking, hustling, connecting or just sharing a new clickbait article to build your social status online? What could boredom possibly offer over all that? But rather than escape boredom, all you do is encourage a greater power of boredom over your brain.

When we run from something, or hide ourselves from it, we avoid confronting issues head-on. We might feel like we have achieved something – I wasn't bored when I had to wait to meet my friend, I was checking my emails! – but what we have in fact done is taught our brain, incident by incident, that boredom is the worst possible feeling and should be avoided by the brain at all costs.

In fact, boredom has many benefits. While we can escape it, it's all around us all the time, almost as much as death, and by encouraging introspection and reflection it encourages creativity and problem-solving. It allows curiosity to develop, as questions form in our minds that would otherwise be drowned out by external inputs. Boredom encourages us to question our lives and what actions have taken us to these points of boredom: do I actually need a new job? Would a different commute be better? Are my evenings not being used in a way that makes me feel good when I go to sleep? The chance to be bored encourages focus and self-control, as our brain's ability to handle boredom is linked to our skills at regulating our own thoughts and behaviours. It even benefits our mental health, giving our brains a valuable moment to breathe without a flood of data and visuals being dropped into it. With all these benefits, why would you deny your mind such an amazing chance to develop and enjoy more of life?

How, then, do we truly enjoy those moments of boredom, or even just simple stillness. What are the ways the Stoics would encourage us to cherish each moment of life? Boredom is the space that allows for introspection.

Never forget that you must die; that death will come sooner than you expect . . . God has written the letters of death upon your hands. In the inside

of your hands you will see the letters M.M. It means
'Memento Mori' – remember you must die.

— JOHN FURNISS

EXERCISE

If you look out of the window, or at the people and nature around you, what can you see? What are the people doing? What about any birds or other animals? What is the light like where you are? What can you hear? Are they man-made or natural sounds? What scents are there in the air around you? Reaching only from where you are sitting, what textures can you feel?

Living is the only time you can experience any of these things. Whatever you are going through right now, you are alive. There are exciting, surprising and beautiful moments all around you, if you make the time and

> opportunity to pause and notice the external
> world beyond the ideas, fears and hopes in
> your head.

This concept of mindfulness and appreciation of course isn't just limited to the Stoics. It appears in most religions and philosophies across the world in one form or another, across time and cultures. Humans clearly understand the value of taking moments in our day to exist purely in that moment, and that accepting our own mortality is what makes these moments so precious. Death itself offers many mysteries: no one knows what happens afterwards or what becomes of those experiences we have had in our lives.

In an old Buddhist story, a man is given a beautiful glass, admired by all, which he uses every day, saying cheerfully each time, 'It's already broken!' One day, the glass is knocked from its shelf and smashes into pieces on the floor, but the man is unperturbed, saying again, 'It was already broken!' The man recognised that he was happy before he had the glass and would be happy afterwards – the glass was merely a drinking vessel and all things must die. As Epictetus said, in what may seem like one of the more extreme Stoic quotes, 'If you are kissing your child or wife, say that it is a mortal whom you are kissing, for thus when they die, you will not be disturbed.' We might struggle with this idea to begin with, but what he said is true – we are all mortal, and everything any of us love will one day be dead. We live so far away from death now for so much of our lives that the shock of mortality is terrifying and extreme. Epictetus is right, that like the beautiful glass, we can enjoy the life that will one day end, and we can hopefully lessen grief by welcoming the reality of death.

Death is inevitable. It is a fact. But perhaps in accepting this truth, we may find that the certainty around death and our own mortality can be a comfort. It is a gift that makes every moment in our life something special, if only we choose to remind ourselves of it daily, and welcome in the habit of Memento Mori.

IN SUMMARY

Remember death.

In the face of death, most of our problems dissipate and we stop caring about the opinion of the crowd.

Your past is over, and your future isn't promised. Enjoy this moment.

CHAPTER 7

Does Anyone Get Me?

or Nature Ties Us Together

I n a world where social media is advertised as connecting everyone, but at a time where everyone feels more divided than ever, it's fascinating to turn to the Stoics' idea of connection. It's impossible to open our phones or watch the news without feeling like our differences are insurmountable, that the arguments raging around us are impossible to bridge and can only lead to the total breakdown of communications, politics and social structure. And yet Stoics believe that the very nature of humanity joins everyone, and everything, together.

We know we won't agree with – or even like – everyone; could any of us name a single person who is 'perfect' to us, with no behaviours we could occasionally do without? We all have habits and opinions that could drive the steadiest spirit into frustration, and we are often encouraged by the forces around us to focus on the differences between us all, but treating people as if we love them benefits us as much as it does them.

And it's not about lying or 'being fake'. It's about practising habits of thought that can develop and strengthen the more we do them. If we focus on what divides us, whether it's our pizza-topping preferences or bigger political issues, we will only see the divisions and differences. But if we get into a daily routine of seeing our connections, that way of viewing the world will become part of us, no longer a habit but instead a new way of being, whatever our current situation in this moment. It's about that idea we've looked at before, *sympatheia*, where we're all tied together by our natures and the simple fact of our existence: really, we're much more connected than we are led to believe.

After hours of scrolling on our phones, it can sometimes seem hopeless to take all the steps necessary to see and engage with people face to face. But a good life involves remembering the connected-ness of humans, and how much we all thrive among those connections. So, if you start considering that instead of people being your potential enemy, every single person in the world is a potential friend or, better yet, a sister or brother in humanity, then we all benefit:

— We increase our own empathy for and understanding of others
— We live in a society where empathy is offered before hostility and suspicion
— We feel more bonded to those other people we see, rather than threatened or alienated
— We experience less fear, anger and self-consciousness
— Our mental health improves because we live in what we see as a safer, closer community
— We do live in a safer, closer community

How does that sound?

Revere the gods and look after each other. Life is short – the fruit of this life is a good character and acts for the common good.

— MARCUS AURELIUS

The Stoics understood that people feel better the more connected they are. They also acknowledged that not everyone will feel the same way or behave according to the Four Virtues. So, how do we get along when others might still be committing crimes or breaking moral codes?

Marcus Aurelius also says in his *Meditations*, 'Men are born for the sake of each other. So either teach or tolerate.' In other words, we are here to help each other out – and part of that means we have a choice to silently accept other people's behaviours, or we have a responsibility to educate them in ways they can do things better and follow the Four Virtues.

In our current Western civilisation, we believe that punishment should follow a crime. But what if, either instead of or alongside, we offered reformation, taking the time to understand why the crime happened, and how we can prevent it happening again for the original criminal or for others who might find themselves in those same circumstances? Reoffending rates are high across most of the Western world, despite prison being a place no one wants to return to – so isn't it time to look at changing our view on those who have done something wrong? Countries like Norway have some of the lowest reoffending rates in the world, and they focus on restorative justice and rehabilitation, working with prisoners to understand what they have done wrong, and giving them the practical tools to make better choices for themselves and their communities. Any justice system, according to Stoic principles, should be about educating our 'enemies' and bringing them closer to wisdom, not increasing the overall amount of suffering in the world.

The responsibility of the Stoic is to teach others to do better, to live according to the Four Virtues, and to offer choices to those not following the Virtues.

So how do we apply that to the day-to-day world?

Man is by nature a social animal; an individual who is unsocial naturally and not accidentally is either beneath our notice or more than human.

— ARISTOTLE

Stoicism can often be interpreted quite differently to the original philosophy. Some people hear 'Stoic' and picture something hard, tough, cold, an isolated island cut off from everything around it, an effective defence mechanism against anything weaker or that might bring a Stoic person down.

But it's a misunderstanding not just around Stoicism, but about humanity. We never thrive when we cut ourselves off. Isolation isn't a strength, but a weakness. Humans couldn't have survived if we isolated the weak from the strong; we are a species that supports, connects with and cares for those who are injured or ill. We learn from older and younger people in our community. We develop ideas together and recover from mental and physical ailments only because we have built trust amongst one another. True strength comes not from cutting yourself off, but from opening yourself up, from letting life pass fully through you and offering no defence. Defence mechanisms are only there because we fear being weak and our weakness being exploited: if we can encourage in our own minds the ideas and habits that others are connected to us, that we are all part of the world together, we not only reduce our need for defence, but we encourage the reality of a connected world too. In the Stoic mind, to refuse our social nature is to be no more than an unthinking beast – and accepting the connection between all people is our real strength. Our existence is down to our ability to work together and has been the key to our survival for hundreds of thousands of years. Asking for help isn't giving up, it's a refusal to give up. We can be wise enough to understand that other people may have the answers, and we can be courageous enough to seek their guidance.

It can be hard to reach out to people; hard sometimes to make small talk and eye contact, to listen to people we might not normally gravitate towards, and to welcome people we fundamentally disagree with. But it also tends to happen that, by their nature, the most unlikely connections can offer us insights, experiences and empathy that we otherwise would not ever have sought because we didn't have the connections to know what we were missing. If we remain in the comfortable company of people who agree with us constantly, we create an echo chamber that means we'll never experience anything new or face the challenges to grow.

EXERCISE

The next time you are out of your home, be aware of feeling any kind of judgement towards someone. Do they alarm you? Do they make you feel self-conscious? Do you feel like they're causing you a problem, or could cause you one?

Take a moment to think of some possible reasons for the behaviours that are registering negatively for you. Could it be that they don't speak your language and are struggling with a sense of communication or place? Could they be extremely stressed, or worried about some news they've received? Could they be deep in their own head, thinking intently about an issue, which is making them present as aggressive or angry themselves? Are you doing any of these things, which may be making others react to you?

Is there a way to recognise your reactions to people and shift them? If you tell yourself a story about the burdens other people could be carrying, does that help to lessen the story of threat or 'otherness' you've previously believed about them? How does that make you feel after just one day of doing this exercise?

We view strangers – and often even the people we know – with our own preconceptions. Whatever day we have had will affect how we perceive those around us. How rarely does a truly happy person believe others around them have bad intentions? And how many times have we had a terrible day, and decided the people we've seen are giving us 'looks' or trying to 'get at us' in some way?

In 2012, the writer John Koenig coined the word 'Sonder' in *The Dictionary of Obscure Sorrows*, his project to come up with terms for those feelings that didn't yet have words for them in English. He described the meaning as 'the profound feeling of realising that everyone, including strangers passing in the street, has a life as complex as one's own, which they are constantly living despite one's personal lack of awareness of it.' Stoicism encourages this realisation, the deep sense that whatever might divide us, the rich internal lives we are living and the very fact of our humanity unite us in a far more meaningful, practical and emotional way.

> The universe made rational creatures for
> the sake of each other, with an eye towards
> mutual benefit based on true value and
> never for harm.
> — MARCUS AURELIUS

Despite our flaws, we are much more rational than we give ourselves credit for. Many of our worst feelings, of fear, anxiety and anger, come from life experiences or the one-off experiences of others that have been shared with us. But it doesn't make those feelings, carried unquestioningly, sometimes for decades, rational in themselves.

As one Tumblr writer once put it, 'If you roll your cart on the same path, it'll soon be the only path you can take.' It's a perfect way of looking at changes we can make to our daily lives: if we only ever think in terms of fear and anger, in no time at all that will be the only way we *can* think, and that will be the 'reality' of our world. But if instead we make that small steer away from suspicion and worry, away from viewing everyone as a potential threat or enemy, we reduce the risk that every day will be filled with suspicion, fear, threats and enemies.

EXERCISE

When did you last witness an act of kindness between one stranger and another? Have you ever practised or experienced an act like this yourself? What effect could this act of kindness have had on both participants' lives?

This week, can you find an opportunity to do an act of kindness for a stranger, like picking something up for someone when they've dropped it, or offering to share your umbrella? How did it make you feel, before and after? Did it give you any sense of how you are connected to those around you? Would you do another act like this in the future?

When I was younger, I struggled so much with my anxieties, and even leaving the house. I was always walking with my head down, convinced other people were looking at me and talking about me, something we now call the Spotlight Effect, where we believe we're noticed much more than we are. But one day, I started seeing people as family-like, people with their own issues, who were sons and daughters, partners, parents, employees and siblings. I realised that whatever I was feeling, they could be feeling too, and actually the whole world didn't revolve around me. Most of the time, I realised with massive relief, no one really thought about what I was doing, wearing or saying. I didn't have to be so incredibly self-obsessed because on the scale of everything, I didn't amount to that much in most people's lives and, in fact, what I could do was try to help people with the things *they* were struggling with.

We are perfectly capable of training some of our thoughts. Often our worries and anxieties are practised: the more we worry, the better we get at it.

The more we dwell on our anxieties, the more they increase and the quicker our brain can access them. If we can get outside our comfort zone and gradually realise the 'unreality' of many of our fears, we can potentially make them weaker and weaker until they disappear. The more we can be present in our own existence, the more we realise that our fears are not needed, and we have the space to engage in what's truly happening in the moment.

> Everything that the Earth produces is created for man's use; and as men, too, are born for the sake of men, that they may be able mutually to help one another; in this direction we ought to follow Nature as our guide, to contribute to the general good by an interchange of acts of kindness.
> — CICERO

Many Stoics believed that the products of the Earth – animals, plants, water – were there for humans to enjoy. But they could never have imagined the power we have had over our surroundings for the last few hundred years, and the effect we've had on those products. So, what would Stoics have thought about man's use of the Earth in this industrialised, globalised world?

The simple metaphors of Stoicism are key here. If you behave poorly to your surroundings, you will have poorly treated surroundings; now, if we abuse our environment with pollution and exploitation, we will have an exploited, polluted environment to live in. Although the ancient Stoics will have been thinking locally, modern Stoics can just size up to a global overview. We are all connected, so whether it is about surroundings – our surroundings are no different, in terms of needing to be cared for and respected, to those surroundings of a citizen of China or Bangladesh or America – or community – those citizens are also in our community of humanity – our Stoic outlook is about ensuring that what is good for us is good for everyone.

Travel blogger Matt Kepnes has noted, 'People really are the same everywhere. Interacting with people, watching them commute, pick up laundry, go grocery shopping, and do all the other everyday things you did back home – you really internalise the idea that, fundamentally, we all just want the same things: to be happy, to be safe and secure, to have friends and family who love us. The how of what we do is different but the why of what we do is universal.' There is a universality about humanity that we often forget: that, in Stoic terms, fire burns upwards, plants grow, animals migrate and feed their young, and the nature of humans is to reason. All humans have it, and all of us are capable of developing it – something some online philosophy proponents struggle with occasionally. I've had some people try to argue with me that women can't be Stoics, and I'm embarrassed that we even need to argue this. Why not ask Porcia Catonis, daughter of Cato the Younger and wife of Caesar's assassin, Brutus, who said of his wife, 'Though the natural weakness of her body hinders her from doing what only the strength of men can perform, she has a mind as valiant and as active for the good of her country as the best of us'? Why not ask Musonius Rufus, who clarified, 'It is not men alone who possess eagerness and a natural inclination towards virtue, but women also. Women are pleased no less than men by noble and just deeds, and reject the opposite of such actions. Since that is so, why is it appropriate for men to seek out and examine how they might live well, that is, to practise philosophy, but not women'? Or Fannia, a first-century AD Stoic who was repeatedly exiled for her support of Stoicism, on whose impending death, Pliny the Younger wrote, 'It grieves me to think of so excellent a woman being torn from all of us, who will never, I fear, see her like again'? Or Elizabeth Carter, an eighteenth-century progressive who was the first ever person to translate Epictetus's *Discourses* into English, and who supported both the Society for Effecting the Abolition of the Slave Trade and the Bluestocking Circle, an early feminist group of women encouraging female education? It's not a real question – of course women are Stoics, as all humans who, regardless of sex, live with reason. To live with that reason, harnessing and practising it, is to live in accordance with what makes humans unique among all other living things.

Role models are vital here too, both in terms of behaviours and actions. Good role models plant the seeds of future good behaviours in those who witness them. While the act of doing good is enough in Stoicism, there is the possibility of those good actions being echoed and spreading in months or years to come. Someone showing us care encourages us to show care to others who need it; someone showing care to Nature and their surroundings both encourages others to continue the behaviour, and for Nature to flourish in that surrounding, getting a foothold to recover and help others to boost flourishing plants and animals around there.

If we can fully absorb the idea that we are one community, with countless opinions and habits, living in one habitat, we open ourselves up to empathy, peace, environmental recovery and improved global health.

IN SUMMARY

We all live in one interconnected existence, and every action ripples out across it.

Decide what you want to put out into the world.

Whatever anyone does or says, I must be a good man. It is as if an emerald, or gold or purple, were always saying: 'Whatever anyone does or says, I must be an emerald and keep my own colour.'

———

MARCUS AURELIUS

CHAPTER 8

Thumbs Up, Thumbs Down

or Good and Evil

As we saw in Chapter 5, Marcus Aurelius was a great man who perhaps failed to be entirely as good as he wished. He used his writings to cope with his awareness of death and his problems with anger, and to strive daily towards his goal of goodness and the Four Virtues.

But he also believed that it was basic human nature to be good, that evil exists and always would, but it was our imperative as Stoics and as humans to know the proper path to eudaimonia, to connect with others and to do the good we can. Doing something seemingly so difficult doesn't mean the effort isn't worth the reward.

Unfortunately, it's easy to be cynical and give up hope. It's an easy step to believe that the world is a mess, nothing good lasts, everything ends and good people have terrible things happen to them. You can believe this, give up hope, and, yes, life is miserable, but it's easy and you won't ever have to strive for anything or risk being proven wrong. It frees you up to live however you want because nothing ultimately matters. That way of thinking can feel horribly comfortable really quickly.

But hope is work, and brave people see the good in life, even when they may not have had good luck themselves. Goodness is work, too. If a 'bad' person wants money, they can steal it or exploit others into getting them money, while a 'good' person doesn't have those options. 'Badness' is easy and requires no moral or internal strength, while 'goodness' requires true fortitude. Think of Ned Flanders in *The Simpsons*, the kind, helpful neighbour to the Simpson family for over thirty years: in some ways, he's a comical fool, always a punchbag for Homer's anger, greed or laziness, but his internal strength and moral beliefs allow him to maintain his life philosophy of goodness, no matter what is thrown at him.

Across a life, everyone mostly faces the same problems, and if we can get through them and still be good, still make choices to put goodness out into the world, that shows an immense kind of strength. In some of the bleakest and hardest situations in human history, there have still been people there displaying and encouraging hope and goodness, generosity and humour, optimism and kindness. If the most nightmarish creations of human evil can still contain humans at their best, what can we do right now in our own lives?

Ned Flanders may be comical against Homer's cynical 'realism', but who's actually having a better time? Homer is filled, episode after episode, with anger, frustration, dissatisfaction and despair, while Ned's life is full of joy, love, goodness and optimism. No matter what Homer throws at him (sometimes literally), Ned believes the best and so is rewarded with the feelings that come with holding that view. Hope and love are not a weakness or a soft option – they require a clear moral philosophy that gives us the tools to see the world as a better place, and one worth bringing more goodness into.

Certain, particularly online, social groups believe that strength comes from taking nothing from anyone. This means isolating yourself to build up your mental strength, removing reliance on others, behaving however you think benefits you the most, positioning others 'below' you and often believing that women are to blame for all events and situations that men in these groups don't like in their lives. By alienating themselves from 'weaker' members of society, they will become the 'strong' men they 'should be'. They are so afraid to be vulnerable that they push away the world and hide their pain with fake confidence, but it hinders them from being the better version of themselves that they could be. It takes a real strength to listen to criticism, and feel the pain of it, to still work on yourself and be open to optimism and joy. How many of these groups would be willing to do that, to make the connections that are exactly what society relies on to build and improve, collectively and individually? It's easy to mock the kind of hard work that Ned Flanders puts into shaping his world into a good place, and it's effortless to leave somewhere worse than you found it – it takes strength and effort to change your behaviour and do the work that makes things better for everyone. But that's the point – it does improve things for *everyone*.

EXERCISE

This is called the *premeditatio malorum* – negative meditation.

Sit down somewhere quiet. Imagine that a really bad thing has happened to you, perhaps something that's a great fear. Maybe that's enough for now – maybe you're able to go further.

If you can, imagine that everything has gone wrong. You've lost everything and everyone you know.

Sit with that for a moment. Allow yourself to accept that everything passes.

Now realise that this thing hasn't happened. Do you feel gratitude for what you still have? Can you practise that gratitude every day? Everything will be lost one day, but doesn't the gratitude offer more opportunity to do good in the world?

Waste no more time arguing what a good man should be. Be one.
— MARCUS AURELIUS

Fred Rogers was an American minister and creator of the educational preschool TV series *Mister Rogers' Neighborhood*, a programme focused on giving children a sense of wonder, curiosity and empathy about the world in which they were growing up. In his Television Academy Foundation interview, he famously said, 'When I was a boy and I would see scary things in the news, my mother would say to me, "Look for the helpers. You will always find people who are helping."' It was advice he created for children, to comfort them in times of disaster, but it's advice that still stands for adults when we're watching global news events that we have no control over; and for a Stoic, we can take that advice even further, to be the practical helpers. During the COVID-19 pandemic, society didn't break down – through hardships and uncertainty, neighbours helped one another, countries rallied around with donations and shared scientific research, and people tried to maintain connections through everything from music played from balconies, to community WhatsApp groups set up to check in on vulnerable members. When the war in Ukraine started, donations came in from across the world in the form of clothing, food, supplies, manpower and money. People want to help.

Of course, it doesn't require a disaster to be a helper. For most people, on most days, we will face no major disaster, but we will experience mishaps, accidents and unkindnesses. We can each choose to do good in those situations, in every one of those situations we come across.

I remember driving once in snow through a town and noticed a gang of kids beside the road, watching the cars skidding about. I thought – remembering what I was like at their age – they were waiting to pelt the cars or their passengers with snowballs, but as I watched I realised they were all waiting to help. In the chaos of the traffic and the weather, they pushed the cars that needed it, behaving calmly and cheerfully, and plenty of cars that would have been stuck there for hours escaped safely home because of those children. I couldn't stop thinking about those kids for weeks, astounded at my misinterpretation and the way they had chosen not to exist in the world as observers of difficulty, but as active participants of goodness using their chance to help. All it had taken was deciding in that moment to just do the right thing. Similarly, I saw a kid waiting at the tram stop, and people were staring at him because of his 'rough' clothes and demeanour. I also made all sorts of judgements about him from his appearance. It took me a moment to register that he was picking up litter, with no one else about encouraging him or checking what he was doing – he was clearly just doing it while he waited for the tram, believing it was the best thing he could do with his time. He's the reason I now pick up rubbish when I go on walks.

Often these good actions cost us nothing, but we still hesitate. What if someone doesn't want help? What if they object to our offer? What if we do it wrong? What if we make it worse? But we remember the offers of goodness we've received, don't we? The times we were desperate, alone and vulnerable, and someone for no reason stepped in and helped us, either practically or emotionally. They had no reason to do it, they didn't want anything in return, it was a simple act of human goodness that probably made our day and stayed with us for a long time after. Maybe it even influenced us to do our own act of goodness in the world, for no reward or strict purpose. A kind comment or smile can stay with us long after the moment passes, just as an unkind gesture does, but that positive gesture of good breaks the spell that the world is a bad place. If the world is so hopeless, why would someone smile at us for no reason?

EXERCISE

This is similar to the exercise in the previous chapter, but this time we're looking at how you can bring goodness into the lives of those around you, rather than strangers.

When you make your lunch, can you make an extra portion to share with someone? Can you offer a lift out of your way to a friend? Could you make a round of coffees for your colleagues, or send a card to someone who you've been meaning to contact again?

Take a moment to think what these gestures might mean to you if you received them.

> Think about the power you have to turn some-one's day into a good one, and what a difference that could make.

In Stoic philosophy, evil exists as the presence of the Four Vices: foolishness, injustice, cowardice and intemperance. As we've discussed before, an object is not good or evil on its own – it's the vices or virtues we perform with it that dictate its status. Money itself is neutral, but if we use it to exploit or abuse people, it becomes a vice. If we spend it on helping others, it's virtuous. But we're much less likely to do 'bad' with a virtue – little harm comes from being too wise, just, courageous or moderate. And conversely, it's a rare good consequence that can ever come from foolishness, injustice, cowardice or intemperance. A person who acts out of vice can never intend to do good, and a person who acts out of virtue rarely performs an evil.

*

As @cryptoseneca said on Twitter, 'It's easy to spot a yellow car if you're looking for a yellow car,' something known as the Baader–Meinhof phenomenon. If your mission is to find a yellow car, suddenly they start popping up everywhere – how did you never notice how many yellow cars there are on the roads? You can always find the thing you're focusing on – where you place your focus, you also place your energy. If you put all your energy into believing the world is a bad place, with bad people doing sinister things and people like you being crushed and pushed out, that's exactly what you'll see. If you view the world with cowardice, foolishness, injustice and intemperance, you'll see those reflected back at you. It's easy to do, but it makes life so much harder for you. You don't get let down, but it lowers your own standards because if everyone is doing it, why can't you?

Think how exhausted you feel when every anecdote you tell after a hard day is about the bad things that happened to you – do you feel better for getting it off your chest? Or is there a larger feeling that something isn't quite right in your world view and you haven't told the right story about what the world really is? As Marcus Aurelius said, 'The soul becomes dyed with the colour of its thoughts.'

I think of the story of two twins, brought up in a home with an alcoholic, violently abusive father. As adults, one twin was an abusive alcoholic with a divorce behind him; the other was a loving father and husband. When asked why they'd turned out that way, they both had the same answer: 'Because my father was a violent, abusive drunk.' Do we want to perpetuate the evil that exists, or do we want to take control of the way we view our opportunities?

EXERCISE
They might be hard to spot at first but try to notice the small acts of good and the pleasures in the world. On your phone or in a small notebook, write down every time you notice

one of these things – maybe it's just a great rainstorm or a single bird or someone holding the door for you in a café for a moment.

Soon you'll start to see them more and more.

Someone at work made a cake and shared it; wasn't that effort kind? Someone on the bus gave you their paper. You didn't get the promotion, but you got some great practice for the next interview you'll do. Your meal got horribly overcooked when you forgot it in the oven, but now you've got a chance to try that takeaway around the corner. And weren't they so friendly when you came to collect it?

After a week, how do you feel when you look at your list? Do you think it's become easier to notice good things in the world?

When really large challenges appear in your life, are you still able to notice the good?

Evil exists, just as good exists. There will always be bad, just as there will always be good. But Stoic philosophy teaches us that accepting badness doesn't have to mean you see the world as a bad, hopeless place – instead, that acceptance means seeing the space you can move into, to practise goodness. And be courageous enough to offer goodness even when it seems unwarranted or unneeded. I remember standing in a shopping centre and watching someone for a minute or two who had fallen down. Shoppers were continuing to stream past them without even slowing down, so I just kept watching, assuming they were already getting help, or didn't need it – maybe wouldn't even want me offering. This is known as the Bystander Effect, where the more people there are, the more people assume that others are better able to help someone in need, and that their own help may be unwanted or even risky. Eventually, I plucked up the courage and went to ask, and they did need a hand; my reliance on the crowd's attitudes had very nearly wrong-footed me completely.

You can remove the power of Evil by knowing you can do Good at every conscious moment. There will always be space for you to do the right thing. Around two thousand years after the original Stoic philosophers, the Scottish writer Robert Louis Stevenson observed this, and suggested, 'Don't judge each day by the harvest you reap, but by the seeds that you plant.'

You can always choose your perspective, and what kind of world you live in.

EXERCISE

Remembering our Stoicism™ game in Chapter 5, imagine every rude person is part of the game. They aren't sent to torment you or personally upset you – they are a type of human, in that moment, known as The Rude Person. They are a naturally occurring phenomenon, a part of humanity as much as birth and death. So just observe them!

Notice what they do, and how they express their rudeness. Is it through anger? Sarcasm? Aggression? You can have no effect on their decisions, but do you have a chance to offer this particular Rude Person any goodness? Can you offer them your seat or ask if they want a cup of tea?

Stoic empathy allows you to understand that this Rude Person simply hasn't yet learnt how to communicate what they're feeling. But this is still an opportunity for you to practise your skills in Stoicism™.

Don't explain your philosophy. Embody it.
— EPICTETUS

We've heard a lot from Epictetus, a Stoic philosopher with a physical disability, who was born into slavery and endured a life full of hardship. After everything he experienced, he chose the Stoic path and became acclaimed as a practical philosopher, embodying his teachings through example, actually living the philosophy he instructed. We have no remaining samples of any writings he may have made – in fact, it is believed his focus was so much on living according to the principles of Stoicism and instructing those around him right in that moment, that the writings of his we do have come solely from students who copied down his words as he spoke them.

But Stoicism has lasted not just in the writings that survived and were passed down. Stoic philosophy continues to be taught – and lived – because it is a philosophy that develops and evolves over time. As was common in their time, some early Stoics kept slaves. Modern Stoics consider the environment and global development, modern psychology and social transformation. Stoicism changes through history because the world changes. But you don't need to know anything about the history of Stoicism to be a true Stoic.

Whenever I remember the binman who gave me that book at the bus stop, I'm struck again at his gesture. He had absolutely no reason at all to notice me, to remember what I was doing each morning, to see the book and connect it to my reading, to pick it up and look after it, and then to find me again and give it to me. There was no cause for any of those things to happen on his part. But he chose to do good, and it's stayed with me for years – who knows how much of that one single action has made me the Stoic I am today.

And remember, as Marcus Aurelius said, 'When you have done a good deed that others have had the benefit of, why do you need a third reward – as fools do – praise for having done well or looking for a favour in return.' Stoics do good deeds because they improve the world, and along with the building of our character, they are the only reward we need. Doing a good deed is its own reward, and if we commit to making this a habit, it'll likely develop into a natural inclination to find opportunities for doing further good. We don't have to look for the good – we can be the good. It will become an instinct, a tendency that perhaps you never thought was part of your character. But you've built your character now, and your developed nature is to do good whenever you can. Go on, and keep building.

IN SUMMARY
Evil exists in the world, and bad things happen to good people.
But you can always make the choice to be good and carry good with you wherever you go.

If someone can prove me wrong and show me my mistake in any thought or action, I shall gladly change. I seek the truth, which never harmed anyone: the harm is to persist in one's own self-deception and ignorance.

―――

MARCUS AURELIUS

CHAPTER 9

You Know that Little Voice in Your Head

or Truth Is Good

We're told these days that there are so many truths, which all deserve respect and equal attention. My truth, your truth, the truth of an observer's feelings. When those truths contradict one another, how can we know which 'truth' to follow?

Marcus Aurelius faced the same issue two thousand years ago. He recognised that truth is a fact of life, something to be sought and discovered, and to ignore or run away from the truth is actively harmful.

We might say now that it's an undeniable truth that someone saying something offensive to us is harmful. But is that really an undeniable *truth*? A Stoic would argue that, in reality, someone saying something 'offensive' to us has two possible roots: a truth that might make us uncomfortable but has the potential to teach us something and improve our life; or it's a lie, and therefore we don't need to pay it any attention. Either way, there's no reason for it to cause us any pain.

If we're totally honest with ourselves and listen to that little voice in our head nudging us towards our better selves, we know that we all hold biases and ways that we invest in situations and people that may be completely detached from reality. We use those biases to make judgements on how to act and react in situations, whether direct (how we treat people) or indirect (how we might think about those people's own actions, even if we have nothing to do with the actions or consequences).

Truth is actually a useful shortcut, a quick route to the reality of any situation. There's that famous expression about truth being somewhere between any two people's versions of it, and that's where we need to find ourselves as Stoics. So, if we're having an argument, the passions and egos of both parties get in the way – we find ourselves wanting to win the argument, and that means we might distort, exaggerate or misremember the truth so our point can be made effectively enough that we can 'win'. But, of course, we're entering that argument with bias, so our focus isn't on getting to a truth that benefits all parties; it's on using any aspect of the original 'truth' as proof so we get what we want from the discussion.

If, however, we try to view the argument from the point of view of a god, with no stake in the debate, we can see things far more clearly. Arguments between friends, family, within couples or between colleagues – these should be engaged with as a disinterested party, someone just trying to get the greatest benefit for all, with clear sight about what has gone before and no ego-involvement to make the conversation spiral out of control. And as a Stoic, we can use these discussions to find our own weaknesses: what could be true about the points made 'against' us? How could we work to build our own character against the flaws that have been shown to us? Is it specific issues raised? Is it our own temper or defensiveness we've discovered in the conversation? Wisdom, after all, is understanding both others *and* ourselves.

> **If it is not right do not do it; if it is not true do not say it.**
> — MARCUS AURELIUS

What is Truth, and how do we find it?

In Stoic philosophy, there are three elements to Truth. Marcus Aurelius said the key to finding truth is to break things down into their absolute simplest form:

1. True Matter

This means, for instance, that wine, even if it's served in beautiful glasses, is still simply fermented grapes. If we take this view over two people arguing, perhaps in our heads it's upsetting, unpleasant, emotional and difficult, but if we break down the reality, an argument is basically two people making noise about a topic they at best don't have 100% full information on or, at worst, are debating only with bad intentions around seeking attention and approval.

2. True Good

This is understanding that the path to eudaimonia, and true goodness in our lives, is to follow the Four Virtues and live accordingly. Stoics are divided over whether or not bad can ever come from good actions, because there can always be unintended and unforeseeable consequences, but Stoicism also says that's no reason to avoid True Good.

3. True Feeling

If we focus on the Virtues, we will naturally discover how to access truth in our day-to-day lives, otherwise known as True Feeling, which is the clarity that enables you to pause when something happens, and to recognise your individual perspective pushing you in a particular direction.

But what if our judgement is flawed? How can we make a reliable assessment if our judgement is imperfect? Particularly now that objective truth – seeing with our own eyes – is no longer a simple matter. Even setting aside our own biases and perspectives, the photos and videos we see online every day are not 'real' but built with editing software and filters. People don't look the way they say they look, their lives are filmed and angled to be perceived positively, their relationships, jobs and holidays are represented in a way that could be miles away from the true facts of them. But seeing the photos and videos inspires reactions in us: reactions of jealousy, of dissatisfaction or of an urge to mimic what we see in our own lives.

We accept so many untruths in our relationships with others and ourselves that perhaps we would not if we could disentangle our emotions and the conflicts between viewpoints. If we see a pair of trainers in a shop that we really like, but discover they aren't in our size, we wouldn't buy them, because the truth of the situation is that we couldn't wear them — they wouldn't be functional as shoes. We could put up with the pain of their being too small or wear more socks if they were too large, but they wouldn't be comfortable. But our bias can get in the way of truth when it comes to partners, friends, colleagues, family. The fact is that our judgement will always be off in one way or another. But by practising True Matter, True Good and True Feeling, and developing our character daily, we build a foundation that offers the chance to reduce the imperfections in our assessments.

> **If anyone tells you that a certain person speaks ill of you, do not make excuses about what is said of you but answer, 'He was ignorant of my other faults, else he would not have mentioned these alone.'**
> — EPICTETUS

Dealing with truth can sometimes feel like hard work. As author and minimalist Joshua Fields Millburn observes, 'People often avoid the truth for fear of destroying the illusions they've built.' I was convinced that to achieve everything I wanted, I had to work seven days a week, over a hundred-hour work weeks, every hour I could keep my eyes open. More work would equal more resources at the other end. Of course, I became exhausted and it took me a long time to recognise that rest would mean I could function much better on my work days. My ego got in the way of the illusion I'd built for myself, and I'd lost sight of Moderation.

Truth is not offensive. It can't be – it's simply a description of what is real. An expression of it may be intended to be insulting, and we can understand that someone is trying to be rude to us, but as in Chapter 4, we merely accept that rude people exist and our job is not to engage with their rudeness. Like the barking dog or the flapping crow, the True Matter of rude people is that they are rude, but that is just the shape of their existence in our lives at that moment. It doesn't mean that they're evil or even that they are trying to upset us; as humans, in a world of high speed, high expectations and high noise levels, we have a tendency to feel annoyance where none is personally intended.

But that doesn't necessarily mean that what a Rude Person is saying might not have truth at its core. Finding Truth in any argument is about collaboration rather than competition. We don't have to 'win' the argument. In fact, the only way to win an argument is to approach it as an opportunity to increase our wisdom and understanding, not to benefit our status. Every debate is a chance for us to find a truth we perhaps hadn't previously considered because we were bound by our foolishness, injustice, cowardice or intemperance – but now we have the opportunity to see a new, more objective truth. Perhaps we *have* been inconsiderate or selfish. This is our chance to see a new truth about ourselves.

EXERCISE

Sitting somewhere you're unlikely to be disturbed, think about the last disagreement you were involved with.

You can probably remember your own viewpoint. Can you remember the viewpoint of the person you were arguing with?

Holding those two views in your mind, can you imagine yourself as someone totally uninvolved in the discussion – a god, or a bird flying over. What would they make of the debate? Could they see what the argument was really trying to achieve? Was there a shared destination you were both missing because your communication was getting tangled? Was the argument a way for one of you to deal with difficult feelings? Was it happening as a way to push the other person away, and the point of the argument wasn't really important at all?

With that distant perspective of the argument, what could each of you have done to make the argument 'successful', and turn it into a calm discussion to guide you both towards where you each needed to be?

> It never ceases to amaze me: we all love ourselves more than other people, but care more about their opinion than our own.
> — MARCUS AURELIUS

We all develop an idea of what happiness or success is. Maybe it's when we're young and having a great time with friends in the park, and someone says they noticed how happy we were that day. It's hard, then, to shake off the sense that this was 'happiness', and when we have another day where we're bored, or grumpy, that we're failing in life because our current feeling doesn't match with that precise one from one occasion someone brought our happiness to our attention.

Maybe it's an idea of friendship or romance that we develop in our minds. I remember watching the classic film *Stand By Me* and really absorbing the idea that this was what friendship looked like, what it was meant to feel like. It took me years to understand that *Stand By Me* not only had an amazing cast of extremely talented actors saying extremely talented writers' words, but also a musical score, a camera crew, lighting team, director, editor, everything. It was a fantasy of what friendship should look like – life doesn't usually have those things. I've been on trips where I've felt it wasn't going as it should because life includes waiting for buses in silence, toilet breaks or someone telling a boring story for too long. Both friendship and relationships can look or feel 'bad' from time to time; there are times when you might have a silly disagreement, or feel that the other person is being thoughtless, and we can often fall into the trap of focusing on how our relationships should look from the outside.

How many people do you know who have put all their energy into making the perfect wedding rather than a good marriage?

But those dull, bad, un-soundtracked moments need to happen to develop us as people, to teach us how to behave with others, to enrich the time we spend together. Any of those 'bad' times might become valuable memories one day, when you feel that your friendship or relationship is nothing like what you see on film or hear in love songs.

We often put so much effort and thought into how others might be thinking or feeling about us. How someone might interpret our clothes, the way we speak up in a meeting at work, how we walk down the street – we may spend hours dwelling on their perspective of us, stressing and worrying about how we can affect their thoughts and feelings. But if we do that, we forget several key truths: that they almost certainly aren't thinking about us (or at least nowhere near as much as we fear), and even if they are, their own interpretation is not objectively 'true'.

It's just an opinion they hold that we have absolutely no control over.

We might all hold these opinions and perspectives, but being bound by them and forgetting how subjective and biased they are can hold us back – through fear, anxiety and preconceptions – from engaging with the world and living most fully.

But if we can practise Stoic habits to remove strong emotions from the situations we find ourselves in, and remember that those emotions don't make our interpretation true, with habit we can start to find those 'difficult' situations far easier to negotiate, and far clearer to see.

IN SUMMARY
Truth does not harm us.
Seek truth and put truth into the world in order to grow good habits.

The essence of philosophy is that a man should so live that his happiness shall depend as little as possible on external things.

———

EPICTETUS

CHAPTER 10

The Truth about Your Wonderful Stuff

or Little Is Truly Needed

We all know that we have too much in our lives. Whether it's stuff – clothes, ornaments, electrical goods, piles of books and trainers and things we'll get round to fixing or selling one day – or plans – the language we'll definitely learn, the place we'll visit eventually, the call we'll make when we get enough time – our lives are defined by the mass of *things* around us and in our heads.

If we think back to Diogenes and his meeting with Alexander the Great (or perhaps that should be the other way around, since Alexander was so much more impressed to meet the philosopher), we remember that this famed thinker could only ask one thing of the acclaimed king and conqueror: 'Move out of the sunlight.'

But why does it benefit us to have less? We like being comfortable, being surrounded by nice things, perhaps even being fashionable. So, what's the harm in having all these *things*?

Everything in our life today encourages us to want as much as possible. Social media, magazines, TV and films – they make us feel that we should at all times either be buying something, or planning how to buy something, and that thing will finally answer our question and fill any hole in our sense of self. We want to feel like we're progressing through life, and the simplest way to feel like we're making progress is through the accumulation and improvement of our things – and once we develop that habit of thought when we're young, it's hard to shift.

We might feel stressed about the work we have to do to earn the money to buy these things, or guilty about the environmental impact of what we're buying, or we might simply recognise that buying stuff isn't making us feel better. So, what do we do to bury those feelings? Focus on the next thing – because *that* will be the one that finally makes us feel good.

*

Every major philosophy and religion recognises that happiness doesn't come from wanting. True happiness comes from feeling that whatever you have is enough. We make ourselves unhappy with all the things we think we should have, and quickly forget that the pleasure we gain when we finally get whatever we've been chasing is short-lived. The pleasure lasts for five minutes, a few hours, maybe, for something major, a few weeks, but it swiftly fades and needs refilling with the pursuit of the next thing.

> **Very little is needed to make a happy life; it is all within yourself, in your way of thinking.**
> — MARCUS AURELIUS

The simple human truth is this: the more we have, the more we want. Looking again at Alexander the Great, he would never achieve what he really sought: a feeling of completeness. The more we surround ourselves with objects and items, the less space we have to realise that the only way to find freedom and happiness is by releasing the urge for those things. When I was younger, I would find myself thinking over and over again, 'There's more to life than what I'm experiencing each day, there's more for me somewhere,' and that became the groove my brain travelled down, all day, every day. It meant that even if I did 'get more', my brain was dissatisfied because the only vocabulary it had for any experience was, 'There's more to life than this.'

We think if we can just get that prize, everything will be fixed and we'll feel completely content in our work, relationships and self. But desire is like a fire within us. To maintain them, fires need feeding, and the more we want, the more our fire is fed, and the more it grows. The more it grows, the more wanting we do, and the bigger it gets. The only way to deal with the fire is to stop feeding it, to let it burn itself out with no fuel, so it will get smaller and smaller until you don't need to feed or watch it at all.

EXERCISE

This is a simple gratitude exercise.

Rather than constantly wondering what more there is to life, always thinking ahead to the moment we'll really start living, let's take a minute to examine the things we already have.

Set aside a few minutes every evening for a week and take a moment to list three things you're grateful for from your day: maybe it's your walk to work, the smells and sights on the way; maybe it's family members who made you feel great that afternoon; maybe it's the meal you ate that evening. What was specifically good about them? What brought you happiness?

Then, can you think of three things you're excited about for the next day: making your morning coffee, seeing colleagues, plans with a friend? Think about what you're really looking forward to about each thing, and what enjoyment you might have when it happens.

By picturing these things and focusing your mind on the pleasure you experienced at each point, you tangibly shift your brain and body, filling it with positive feelings and increasing your habit of finding the good moments of your life. The more you practise this, the more ingrained the habit will become. And after a week has passed, you'll feel the benefits of the exercise and will be well on the way to appreciating the good things you have in life much more.

Take a moment to understand that these small things are enough, that they make up the hours of your life and by finding the best of each day, you remind yourself how good your time as a whole actually is. It's the fuel that will power an enjoyment of life.

In our current culture, it can feel that buying or wanting to buy is an expression of happiness, that everything we want is a rung up the ladder that will bring us closer to happiness. What if just wanting those things is actually an expression of our unhappiness with ourselves – that we are not cool enough, fashionable enough, unusual enough, creative enough, rich enough? Constantly wanting is a statement not that we don't have enough, but that we are not enough in ourselves, and acquiring those things will finally fill a hole, change who we are and improve us without our having to do anything but hand over money. And if we only think about who we'd like to be, how will we ever know our true self, and what we could be capable of?

But how would things look if we changed our habits to become the person we wanted to be instead? If we focused on hobbies or fitness or health, the Preferred Indifference choices (we'll come to exactly what that means shortly) and the eudaimonia path of the Four Virtues? In *The Tao of Pooh*, the author Benjamin Hoff talks about how we pervert progress by acquiring more and more things – we think we're getting somewhere by collecting objects and goods, but whether they're honey jars or sports cars, the wanting, getting and lack of satisfaction only get in the way of making ourselves happier and more fulfilled. The people we see online with everything – they aren't better than us at life. They're just better at marketing their lives. Social media is a public display of a need for attention, curating and filtering our lives to get the most eyes on us, which is the new global currency of success. If we have happiness, we don't need this attention, but if we chase the attention, we'll never find the happiness we're after. I know I've been guilty of it in the past, appearing happy in a photo that I now look at and can only remember how miserable and worried I really was. The facade worked, but the effort to appear 'successful' didn't make me feel better, because I was chasing after the wrong thing, only thinking about how I was supposed to appear.

In fact, we make less and less space for our minds and our spirits the more we focus on 'getting'. In the story of the student's teacup, a Buddhist student sits with his master as his master performs the tea ceremony. But as the student's cup fills up, he grows alarmed as the master keeps pouring. The tea fills the cup, then pours over the edge, onto the table and spills further and further. The student calls for him to stop, and the master does, saying, 'This is like your mind. How can you learn if you continually pour in more desires and thoughts into your mind? You must remove the excess so you can be open to your purpose.' There is a point in all our lives when the amount of 'stuff' we have means that there is no room for the things that actually bring us joy: things like human connection, learning, discovery and creativity.

Marcus Aurelius came from an extremely wealthy family and lived a life of privilege and comfort. In the very earliest pages of his *Meditations*, he recognises the values his mother, a woman very wealthy in her own right, had passed down to him, saying in his thanks, 'From my mother: piety, generosity, the avoidance of wrongdoing and even the thought of it; also simplicity of living, well clear of the habits of the rich.' Even as he lived among them, he recognised the dangers of becoming hooked on the trappings of the very wealthy, warning later, 'Beware of becoming Caesarified, dyed in purple. It does happen. Keep yourself simple, good, guileless, dignified, unpretentious, devoted to justice, pious, kind, affectionate to others and resolute in carrying out your proper tasks.' I'm sure you know people who aren't on any social media, who might have a battered old car and few fancy clothes. Are they unhappier than anyone with a thousand or a million followers? Do they seem content with the things that give them their own individual, unpublished joy? Marcus Aurelius knew, just as we must recognise now, that simplicity, dignity, unpretentiousness and prioritising goodness and justice over Caesar-like objects and fashions is the only path to peace and happiness.

It is not the man who has too little, but the man who craves more, that is poor.
— SENECA

We might follow people on social media for all sorts of different reasons – envy, jealousy, 'hate follow-ing' – but why not follow instead those people who bring you genuine enjoyment, education, value and humour? I've previously been engrossed in a social media life, obsessed with how other people lived and what they had, and it only ever really made me feel bad after scrolling for hours.

A few years ago, I felt like I *had* to have access to social media, that I'd be missing out on knowing things or seeing things if I got rid of my account, but then I travelled abroad for a while and didn't really have the money for a phone and the international contract. I decided to take only an iPod with me and rely on internet cafés when I needed to get in touch with people back home – I'd read so many travel books that the romance of travelling with no phone and just a pack of cards to entertain myself and any friends I made appealed to me. I didn't want to load myself with more stuff when the whole point of going abroad was to enjoy the glut of new people I'd meet and experiences I'd have. It was also part of a growing sense I had of wanting to make my whole life lighter, so I travelled with just a small hiking bag, my toiletries and a few clothes.

It was so wobbly for those first few days, and I realised what a habit it had become for my brain and my hands, using social media as a comfort blanket every time I was bored, or anxious, my fingers automatically swiping to open each app in an endless cycle. I used social media apps every moment of my life like some people go on their phone while watching a film – distracting myself, not engaging properly with anything and getting no real enjoyment either. I always regretted it, but I kept doing it. But after two weeks, I had the strange realisation that I didn't miss it at all. I wasn't actually missing out on anything. If anything, I suddenly had more spare time and more brain space because I wasn't filling it with hundreds of images and words that had no purpose other than to hold me there. My lack of luggage felt amazing too – with only one bag and just a few items, they were so easy to care for and look after. It was just a matter of keeping things clean and dry and neatly folded, and travelling around became so easy. The lack of attention I had to pay to my stuff and my phone freed up my mind so much that I felt I could finally think clearly.

When I got back nine months later to my home and my phone, I wondered about going back on social media and realised a switch had been flicked in me in that time away, where I didn't care about that online world any more. I hadn't missed it. I didn't have any inclination to relapse and I felt no pressure to follow, or not follow, to get angry or envious or disapproving. If I did go back on, it was for discovering those pockets of positivity on the internet, and only for a handful of minutes each day.

The goal of social media companies is to get *and keep* our attention. And attention isn't kept by making us feel good. Social media sites use outrage and envy to get us engaged, then drive dopamine hits from likes and comments to keep us hooked, offering similar highs to recreational drugs and gambling. The US Addiction Center says, 'Addictive social media use will look much like any other substance use disorder.' It goes on to list signs of social media addiction, including mood improvement when the user gets to access it, an emotional and behavioural preoccupation with it, an increasing use over time, physical and emotional withdrawal symptoms, conflict when a user can't access social media, and a reversion to high usage when they've had a break from it. Does this sound like anyone you know? Does it sound like you?

The social media companies don't want us to be discerning, to be aware of the time that's passing; they don't want us to feel any friction at all that might jolt us out of their sites, which is why they now all have endless scrolling and alerts that ping at just the right moment to embed addictive habits. By joining in the endless scrolling, we hand over our most precious commodity – our time (not to mention our data and attention). No one's happy doing unpaid overtime at their job, and yet that's what we do when we go on social media: we hand over our time for *their* profit. How could that possibly bring us happiness? As the software and hardware become ever slicker and more integrated, the tech companies want us to feel that they are offering us everything we could possibly need, often before we know we need it. A tour of a distant gallery you'll never be able to reach in real life? A front-row seat at a sold-out concert from the comfort of your own home? A massive multiplayer game with the chance to play with people all over the globe? How can you turn down these opportunities! Only . . . what if they've sold us those ideas so successfully that we've forgotten what actually makes us happy? And not just happy in the moment, the easy decision over something slightly more hard work where we'd have to get showered and dressed and leave the house – what if the marketing of these online experiences that brings them billions of dollars and world-defining levels of our personal data also makes us forget that the happiness we get from going for a walk locally, making brief conversation with a fellow regular at a coffee shop, helping someone up some steps with a buggy, offering a friend company on a dog walk, just sitting and staring out of the window – all of these things press a button somewhere deeper inside us that we've lost sight of completely.

As we moved as a business into putting out films online, I realised I needed to have a social media account again. It took me a long time to work out how to make it work for me, but when I eventually came back I only followed Stoic accounts and film-making accounts, and suddenly opening up the apps was about short bursts of enjoyment and education, and every occasional visit left me feeling like my life had been improved, not drained.

Besides setting timers for myself that restrict what apps I can use, when I use them and how long I use them for, I make sure I take full advantage of the apps' wanting to give you exactly what you want. I don't let any click-bait titles suck me in, but let the apps know I'm not interested in anything that gives me a dopamine hit, instead just whittling my feed down to filmmaking and Stoicism, and only watching those things that genuinely bring value to my life. I've also heard a great tip called the Shopping Mall Rule: to only follow those people that you would make the effort to go over and speak to if you saw them out at the shops. Why would you give your life over to the lunches and bathroom decoration of people you wouldn't even be pleased to speak to if you saw them in real life?

Finally, I try to keep my phone out of physical reach. Whether it's in another room (when I'm working) or just the opposite side of the one I'm in, I find that having to actively get up to reach it provides just enough resistance that I end up enjoying my phone-free zone. It's amazing the difference we can see if we keep a phone-free zone around where we spend most of our waking time in our homes, and have books, notebooks or puzzle books there instead.

I've also been thinking recently about trying to leave the house more without my phone. If I've left it behind when I've stepped out to go to the corner shop or on a short drive, I feel panicked, like I've somehow accidentally tried to go out without shoes on. But a phone doesn't protect our fragile skin like shoes, or provide social decency like clothes, or keep us alive like vital medication or medical equipment. So, why do we feel so incredibly lost when we go without it for even ten minutes? Something's definitely gone wrong, there.

As countless philosophers and country singers have observed, the good things in life don't come easy. But perhaps we've forgotten the sheer joys that can be found in discovery, resilience, effort, spontaneity, connection and conversation.

EXERCISE

In Chapter 6, we looked at halving our phone time.

Once you have managed to cut down on your time, how about deleting some of the social media apps?

What's stopping you? What do you think you might miss out on?

Perhaps the more important question is what could you be missing out on by being on those apps? What opportunities could be passing you by when your eyes and ears are focused on your phone?

Try it for one week. How do you feel?

How does it feel after two?

What's stopping you from never going back on social media again?

All human beings seek the happy life, but many confuse the means – for example, wealth and status – with that life itself. This misguided focus on the means to a good life makes people get further from the happy life. The really worthwhile things are the virtuous activities that make up the happy life, not the external means that may seem to produce it.

— EPICTETUS

It's useful to remember that saying yes to things is also saying no to other things – we might have FOMO, that fear of missing out, or we might have an urge to buy those trainers because they could sell out and we're convinced they'll make our life better. But every time we say yes to bringing something into our lives, we're also saying no to *not* having it – not managing with the shoes we already have, not having a quiet week at home while our friends are away, even not using up our boring fridge leftovers in a creative way. Making our decisions based on an urge to say yes or no because of our urges and instincts won't build our characters – but considering instead the Four Virtues or even Preferred Indifference means that we avoid illusion and ego and can build good habits that benefit us much more in the long run. So, what is Preferred Indifference?

As we've discussed before, everything that isn't the Four Virtues or the Four Vices comes under Indifference – things that are neither inherently bad nor inherently good, like money, health, ambition, strength and skills. These things neither take away from nor add to the quality of our lives in and of themselves, they are just aspects that we must use within the Four Virtues framework to make a happy life. But there is such a thing as Preferred Indifference and its opposite, Dispreferred Indifference. For example, poverty is neither good nor bad, but we recognise that it can make life more difficult and restrictive, so we would try to shape our lives away from it. Conversely, we generally want to live for longer and feel healthy, so we see health as one of the Preferred Indifferences.

Having said that, though, some circumstances might make it more virtuous to select the Dispreferred Indifference – if our money is coming from a corrupt source that could hinder or damage us in the long run, we may find it wiser and more courageous to opt for poverty over wealth. And sometimes the Dispreferred Indifference is actually beneficial to us – for instance, some kinds of pain can build our strength (in the gym) or tell us when something is wrong with us (an injury or illness). It's really only when the Four Vices begin to shape those Indifferent things that they tip from preferences to things we should avoid. Our lives are short, and we frequently 'need' so much less than we think to be happy, comfortable and content.

EXERCISE

Let's swap our expectations for appreciations.

When we want something, we're putting off our happiness until we gain that thing. But if we sit in a single moment and focus instead on what we have right now, we develop the mental muscle to see all the things we have, and the benefits and enjoyments we get from them day to day.

It is not about the pursuit of more, but about the appreciation of existing. What were you expecting from today that may not have lived up to your expectations? And can you write a longer list of the appreciations you could have for the day? Right now, what can you be grateful for?

IN SUMMARY
The more we take, the more we want.
Enjoy simplicity – it's perfect.

The happiness of your life depends upon the quality of your thoughts.

———

MARCUS AURELIUS

CHAPTER 11

Put on Your Rose-Tinted Glasses

or Thoughts Create Reality

Shakespeare had Hamlet speak a great Stoic truth when he said, 'There is nothing either good or bad, but thinking makes it so.' We shape the world around us by how we think about it, and we need to accept that if we look for badness in the world, we will find it – there's no shortage of evidence to make us feel that this world is hopeless, broken, a source of despair. But we can redefine our lives by building routines of good thoughts, good actions and good habits that seep into how we live and thus how we see the world. In every situation, if we look for conflict, a chance to defend ourselves and an argument, we will find that our lives are full of huge incidents and terrible, unforgivable rows. It's not about our luck, or misunderstandings with the world against you – I remember so clearly when I was working as a bricklayer, getting the bus home and walking down the alley to the house, saying to myself in my head, 'This is rubbish, my life is rubbish.' I suddenly had the strongest sense of these being the only words my brain could produce, and also like I was standing on a stage in front of a crowd, reciting these things so I could convince them how terrible my life was.

At that stage, I hadn't ever made a decision about my life: I'd had to go to school, and hadn't cared about doing or not doing anything there, then when a teacher spoke to me about what I'd do when school finished, they suggested bricklaying and I hadn't cared either way, so I went along with it. In that moment, I realised that if I kept reciting this terrible life situation to myself, I wouldn't have to make any decisions about my future, either, because everyone was so bad and my situation so hard that I couldn't possibly improve anything about it. I could just keep on being angry and miserable, constantly backed up by my internal monologue endorsing how I simply couldn't do any better.

It's quite addictive, though, that sense that we're right about our worst fears, that we don't have to worry about failure because it will never go right for us anyway, that our instincts and conclusions never need to be challenged, that we don't have to experience discomfort, that we never have to admit being wrong, that we don't have to try. Like a friend saying to us, 'Well, you tried your best, don't worry about it,' we can opt out of effort and struggle, just release the pressure and go down the path of least resistance – the most natural of all human instincts. But what happens at those moments in life where pressure, challenge, discomfort and error are the things that help us grow, teach us lessons and open us up? What do we miss out on when we seek comfort at all moments instead?

It's part of our evolution that we latch on to the bad things, whether it's the one piece of criticism after a hundred compliments, or the 'funny look' as we're leaving a good day at work. Human brains benefited by being alert to things that broke patterns or made us feel uncomfortable as a way to mark dangers and respond accordingly. But while our nervous systems might still be wired for tens of thousands of years ago, the world has moved on – we live in large communities in a wider society, with most of us lucky enough to have secure ways of getting food (go to a shop, pay money, walk away with supplies) and shelter (pay rent or mortgage and bills, stay in the same property each night). We don't have to worry about competition for resources in the same way as we did when our brains began evolving towards what we have now, but no one has bothered to pass that message on to our internal systems. So, we're still flagging up and holding on to the one bad comment, the one hostile look, even though we have more than enough reason to understand that the 'bad comment' could be a misunderstanding and the 'hostile look' could be because someone is thinking of something entirely different as they happen to pass us. Our reason is the muscle that has to be worked as we face these conflicting signals, getting into the habit of perceiving the world not as a potential enemy, but as the connected whole that contains everything we know and that knows us.

In that alley, I suddenly thought: why don't I think of good things, instead? Why don't I make the effort to view my life positively? It didn't mean I had to *change* anything in my life, that seemed way too hard at that stage, but I could at least change the story I was telling that crowd in my subconscious. And it was hard to make that shift, to catch myself still thinking negatively, then turn it into something positive in my mind. And then I felt guilty for betraying the young man who wanted reassurance that his life was terrible and he couldn't do anything about it. But it became a habit, after a while, and I gradually began to see that I did have choices where before there hadn't seemed to be any. Instead of feeling like I was facing a high glass wall, and I couldn't get equipment, or deal with my fear of heights, suddenly I was at the bottom of a rock face full of handholds, ready to start climbing.

EXERCISE

Sit somewhere quiet and think about something that happened, whether several years ago or several weeks ago, that you felt was strongly negative at the time – perhaps you lost a job, a relationship broke down or you were forced to move out of your home.

Do you still think it was a negative overall in your life? Did any good come out of it? Could the good things in your life right now have happened if that 'negative' event hadn't occurred?

Next time a 'bad' thing happens in your day, however small, take a minute to think how it could turn out for the best, or what you could learn from the experience.

Thoughts Create Reality, the subtitle of this chapter, is a key part of living as a Stoic. It's easy to confuse this concept with other current 'positive thinking' ideas, but the differences between them are really important to note:

WHAT THIS ISN'T (Part 1):
Totally Unattractive

There's plenty of conversation around positive thinking. You might have heard of the Law of Attraction, most famous from a book called *The Secret*. In the Law of Attraction, the idea is that all you have to do is think positively about experiences and things, and those experiences and things will be brought into your life by the universe. This is not what the Stoic idea of thoughts creating reality is about.

For Stoics, the collection of things and experiences is not the way to live a happy and fulfilled life, nor does a Stoic believe that they know what is best for themselves over a lifetime. The Law of Attraction aims to get you whatever you want, whether it's power and relationships or a new outfit and job, and particularly focuses in its marketing on 'wealth enhancement'. As we've discussed, money itself is an Indifferent, but focusing time and effort on the building up of wealth while not focusing on the building up of character would tend towards the foolish in Stoic philosophy.

The Law of Attraction makes us concentrate, deliberately and purposefully, on what we want – picturing it, imagining it, seeing how good it would feel to have it. If you think achieving wealth and power grants happiness, again: do the rich and powerful seem like the happiest people in the world?

In Stoicism, thoughts are understood to shape the person we are, and how we perceive reality and act within it. We know that we can't shape reality according to our desires, only that we must accept it and behave the best we can when faced with it. We don't control our outcomes and how much we're objectively benefiting; we just control our opinions and our motivations. For instance, two people can receive the same thing but have entirely different feelings about it – one might have temporary excitement and pleasure, while the other experiences guilt and concern. Is it the object causing those feelings or the thoughts around the reality of the object?

WHAT THIS ISN'T (Part 2):
The Poisonous Positives

Another buzz-phrase we hear a lot around mental health and well-being is 'toxic positivity'. This is the idea that we should hide or repress any negative feelings, experiences and reactions, that expressing them means we're dwelling on them and the only way to be happy is to shut down the negative and solely focus on the positive.

Stoics recognise that bad things happen; Stoicism sees the problems in life and understands that the way to deal with those bad things is to confront them, deal with them and find the route through them using the principles of the Four Virtues. We can remove negative bias and perspective and still understand that there is a 'problem' – we can now just see the issue with more clarity and objectivity. So: traffic is still traffic and it might make us late – but Stoicism recognises that we might as well spend time in that traffic listening to podcasts we enjoy. Stoicism doesn't make the storm go away, but it does help you to enjoy running out into the rain. Toxic positivity demands that when issues crop up, we put our fingers in our ears, close our eyes and whistle until we've stopped thinking about it. But what can we learn in those moments? How can I grow through the difficulty? What is life teaching me if I tune out every lesson?

In 2014, the actor Jim Carrey gave a Commencement Speech at the Maharishi University of Management. In it, he spoke to the graduates about the joys of seeing the world as it truly is, the freedom it can bring and the choices we can make, saying: 'Your need for acceptance can make you invisible in this world . . . We are not the avatars we create, we are not the pictures on the film stock, we are the light that shines through. All else is just smoke and mirrors . . . I've often said that I wish people could realise all their dreams and wealth and fame, so they could see that it's not where you're going to find your sense of completion.' He added, with great Stoic spirit, 'When I say life doesn't happen to you, it happens for you, I really don't know if that's true. I'm just making a conscious choice to perceive challenges as something beneficial so that I can deal with them in the most productive way.'

EXERCISE

This is a classic cognitive behavioural therapy technique called cognitive distancing. In the previous exercise, we looked at how a 'negative' experience could actually turn out to benefit you. This exercise focuses instead on how some things might never seem to have a beneficial aspect, but they might still be experiences that you can heal from.

When something difficult comes into your life, ask yourself, 'Will I be over this tomorrow?' Sometimes, all it takes is a good night's sleep.

But that might not be enough. Ask again, 'Will I be over this in a week?'

Maybe not.

'Will I be over this in six months' time?'

Perhaps that still might not be long enough.

'Will I be over this in five years' time?'

And maybe not even then.

'Will I be over this in twenty years' time?'

It might take that long, but perhaps you can see that there will be a day when you will be over this difficult time. Not that you've forgotten it, but that it no longer troubles you in the same way it does today.

This is just a moment, and all things will pass.

> Objective judgement, now, at this very moment.
> Unselfish action, now, at this very moment. Willing
> acceptance – now, at this very moment – of all
> external events. That's all you need.
> — MARCUS AURELIUS

Two men visit a famous monastery in a distant village, determined to meet the wise monk and move to his area. On meeting the wise monk, the monk says to the first man, 'What's your village like?' The first man thinks for a moment, then says, 'Terrible. Terrible people, terrible area. What's this one like?' The monk says to him, 'Bad. You should probably avoid it.'

When the first man has left, the monk says to the second man, 'And what's your village like?' The second man thinks too, and answers, 'Wonderful. It's full of great people doing good things with their days in a beautiful place.' The monk says, 'I think you'll like it here too.' Our thoughts create the reality we live in – if we're convinced everyone around us is awful, those are the people we'll find. If we live in the belief that most people tend to be good overall, then we'll find those same people wherever we go.

I remember staying in a hostel abroad on my own. I was in a shared room, grouped with half a dozen young French guys, none of whom spoke to me or engaged with me in any way. I felt self-conscious, aware that this group of people who knew each other and didn't speak my language were ignoring me, becoming ruder and ruder as the days passed. I felt despair that I'd opted to stay here on my own and thought the whole trip had been a terrible mistake. Then one evening, something came up – I was cooking risotto and one of them wanted to know my recipe, and suddenly this group and I were talking, laughing together, and by the end of the night we were great friends. I'd lost sight of the fact that in my solitary silence, I looked just as rude to them, failing to even try speaking to them and giving off a really hostile vibe. I'd shut down any opportunity to engage with them and connect because the story I'd told in my head was so truthful and deafening to me in that moment.

Nothing had changed between the previous days and that evening, except my opinion and perception. They hadn't objectively become nicer people, and neither had I – we'd each just had the opportunity to set aside our negative impressions until we could actually communicate and realise how much enjoyment there was to be had there.

Similarly, when I was younger I was convinced that the security guard at the local corner shop had it in for me. He was a giant with a mean-looking face, and just stared at me when I went in and nodded to him – it was obvious he hated me. But one morning I decided I'd greet him properly and actually say 'Good morning' when I went in, to be friendly no matter what his response – and a few days later, he became the friendliest man in the world. I realised he came from Poland, and he was probably just as shy about speaking English to me as I get when I have to speak Hungarian to family abroad. I know I clam up and could potentially come across as rude or stand-offish, but it's about my lack of the language, not about my attitude to those around me. He and I became cheerful friends each time I went in because I'd decided to approach him positively, rather than with aggression or defensiveness. 'What are you looking at?', or any equivalent, is always going to be an uphill battle to turn into an uplifting, connecting conversation.

When I think of that bin man who gave me a book all those years ago, I think of how his kindness shifted my whole perspective of the world. Life is uncontrollable, but how I viewed it affected my experience completely and totally.

As Marcus Aurelius says, 'People seek retreats for themselves in the countryside, by the seashore, in the hills, and you too have made it your habit to long for that above all else. But this is altogether unphilosophical, when it is possible for you to retreat into yourself whenever you please; for nowhere can one retreat into greater peace or freedom from care than within one's own soul.' In other words: wherever you go, there you are. You can't run away from your stresses and fears, because you carry them inside your mind;

like the first man visiting the monastery, if we feel the world is rude and hostile, wherever we go we'll find that hostility. But if we perceive the world as always ready to smile back at us, that's what we'll find too.

EXERCISE

Sit in a room and look around you. How many red objects can you see? Consider each one, its texture, weight, size.

Now focus on this page, and don't look around you again yet. How many blue objects were in the room?

The more we focus on one aspect of our life, the more blind we become to others.

Next time you step outside, try to notice three positive things. Are there trees or birds nearby? Does a neighbour say hello? Are the roads clean? Is there a pleasant cooking smell coming from a nearby house? Are your shoes comfortable, or is your coat keeping

---

you warm? Have you been able to drink some clean, fresh water today? Do you have a pleasant feeling from some food you enjoyed just before you left?

As you continue your day, how many other good things can you notice? After trying this a few times, do people seem any different to you when you encounter them at work, on your commute, in the street?

IN SUMMARY

You notice what you're looking for.

The world happens as it does, but you can choose the lens through which you view it.

He is a wise man who does not grieve for the things which he has not, but rejoices for those which he has.

———

EPICTETUS

CHAPTER 12

Don't Stop Stopping

or Be Present

L ife, it turns out, is not so complicated. In fact, it's so much more manageable than we ever imagined. It's not our complex, tangled pasts, and it's not our unknowable, infinite futures. Our lives, the lives of all of us, actually look like this:

............................●............................

The large dot is where we are now, right now, and the dotted line is nothingness, where we had existed and where we might continue to exist. Just stop for a moment and sit with that thought. Can you hear things around you? Is there anyone nearby? How do you feel, in your body? That is all life is. In a few minutes, you will have a different moment – your body will be older, your surroundings will be different, as the whole world is a few minutes changed from before. How is that moment different?

The point is, there is no other moment than the one you are in. There is nowhere else we exist than right now. We don't exist in the past, or the future, in memories or in plans. They are just projections of ourselves, images in our minds that we can feel and remember. We can dwell on 'the good old days', and spend hours thinking about how much better things were, either for us or in the wider world – but were we truly happy then? Did we ever live in a world free from fear? Was the evening news ever cheerful and full of harmless information, and did we live in communities where no one was ever hungry, or frightened, or suffering? And if instead we disappear into the future – 'If I do this, then that will definitely happen and everything will be fixed' – will that make today better? Is 'the future' any more real than any other fantasy in our heads? Is every plan for the future anything more than a distraction from the moment we live in right now? When we think back with fond memories to the past, can we not remember how much we longed for our better future at the time?

We have grown so terrified of boredom that we rush to fill every moment with something else – the second we aren't being immediately stimulated with a conversation, a TV programme, a pressing task, we reach for our phones or a remote control to fill our eyes and sense with something loud and bright and new (and sometimes we even do it when the conversation, programme or task is still continuing, such is our instinct to be overstimulated). We know, truly, when we can stop and think without distraction that we won't look back fondly on all the time we distracted ourselves and pulled ourselves back and forth trying to live in the past or the future, but we allow so little time for ourselves to live in our moments. To-do lists, regrets, plans, corrections; we put ourselves everywhere but Right Now, Right Here.

If you were told that you had to spend all of your waking free time staring at your phone, pressing the screen frequently, would you be happy with your quality of life? Yet we hand over our time on Earth as if we have infinite hours to exist in, and limitless consciousness so we can afford to pour it all away. As we've discussed, attention is the global currency right now. The people in power want our attention because they can turn it into money, but by giving them our attention, we hand over our present moment – which is all any of us ever have. These corporations are stealing our lives, moment by moment, and the only way we can engage with their actions is to consider that the companies' profits are mainly provided by encouraging the Four Vices of foolishness, coward-ice, injustice and intemperance, and we need to con-sider our eudaimonic path. There's a famous question that circulates online about our time and our screen lives: 'You have $86,400 in your account and some-one steals $10 from you. Would you be upset and throw all of the $86,390 away in hopes of getting back at the person who took your $10? Or move on and live?' The point is that we have only 86,400 seconds each day, so why should we throw away our entire day because of one negative moment within it.

We all want to be happy, and it can feel like we're doing the responsible thing when we make decisions to change our lives to achieve greater happiness. Maybe it's about changing our job, or getting out of a relationship, or starting a new hobby or fitness plan. But if we aren't doing it right now, are we doing it at all? We promise ourselves we'll be happy when our changes start, but if we aren't happy with what we have at this moment, why would we be happy with what we might potentially have on another day? We put such hope into our futures, imagining the time when we'll have the skills we want, the home, the job, the body, the relationship. Everything is put into the hope that one day everything will be 'fixed', yet not even 1% of that hope and effort is put into making that future person the one we are right now. Zen teacher Charlotte Joko Beck, who focused on facing anger, anxiety and self-centeredness in her Zen practice, said, 'What makes it unbearable is your mistaken belief that it can be cured.' We are told over and over in our lives that things are to be overcome, to be triumphed against, to be changed and improved – and if we don't do that, we've failed. But what if those ideas only lead to more unhappiness, which comes from our expectations and imaginings more than from the reality we're experiencing. Another Zen student, the writer John Tarrant, talks about the Zen understanding of difficulties in life: 'Suffering is not an anomaly but a clue to freeing the mind. In this sense suffering is not accidental or a mistake, but an enormous beginning. It's the gift that starts a great transformation in our point of view.' He goes on to propose that we ask ourselves, 'What if this is it?' It's not about nihilism or hopelessness, but about actively discovering what he calls 'a profound goodness inside the common life we have.' What we have is now; the only tools we have to deal with this moment are the tools we have on us right now – a little courage, a little wisdom, a little moderation, a little justice. We do the best we can with what we have and use this 'right now' to build our character and carry us on to the next 'right now'. Why would we spend so much time focusing on possible happiness at the cost of today's happiness?

There's a hard path at any given moment that could benefit us as we either push through the current difficulty and build our character, or sit in the moment and learn to savour the emotions and experiences we're living in. Most of our fears and worries disappear completely when we accept the truth that the only moment we live in is the current one, and the vast majority of the time those fears don't exist there. We might dread something 'small' – a visit to the dentist, a presentation at work – or something huge – potential global conflict, climate disasters – but how many of these things are happening right now, and how much of our lives do they take up when they happen?

EXERCISE

Sit quietly and be present.

Accept that just existing in this moment is enough.

Do you find it hard? What is your instinct to do? Do you want to pick up your phone? Are you making lists in your head of what you should or could be doing? Why do you think you find this so difficult?

Set a timer and see if you can do thirty seconds.

Over a week, can you build up that time? Enjoy sitting peacefully and enjoying existing in the moments that make up your life.

It's a common impulse these days to want to be busy, in one form or another, and to keep our minds busy. That comes from our wonderful human instinct to make connections and discover new answers to things, but that superpower gets pushed down the wrong path when we have a smartphone in our hands. Instead of talking to people in the village square or experimenting with things in our garden or our kitchen, that instinct gets pushed into doom-scrolling or mindless bingeing on streaming TV. Imagine if our curiosity and hunger for stories didn't have those twenty-first-century outlets; if we only had journals and sketchbooks, neighbours and family, what could we discover about each other? What could we discover about ourselves?

When we go for a long walk or a hard run it feels fantastic. We have no screen time and no emails, and the tiredness means our focus is on putting one foot in front of the other, just existing in that moment. Our minds are clear, our thoughts are simple, and we often say, 'That felt so good, I must do it more.' Then we see a work email, or we remember the fridge needs cleaning, and our minds are full again of the upcoming task. We lose sight of the simple pleasure of living in our moment. And in addition to the many reasons reading is beneficial for us, the fact that reading can improve our brain structure, increase our empathy levels and literally make our brains feel like we've had life experiences beyond our own, reading a book now is also a form of meditation. If we can sit still for an hour and only look at our book, no phones, no other screens, we are calming and soothing our brains by focusing on a single, slow activity that allows our minds to expand and focus at the same time. Daily, our focus will continue to improve.

The questions that have driven humanity for tens of thousands of years, about what our purpose might be, why we do particular things, why we have inclinations to and from certain ideas or groups or practices – how often do we allow ourselves time to ask those questions? In today's world of instant-aneous results and algorithmic answers, we rarely have the space to live in the moment and sit with the same question – without an answer – for min-utes at a time, let alone the hours, weeks, years that it can take to come up with a new, deep, thoughtful solution that can push human development for-ward. We know that we thrive when we can dwell on questions for a long time, giving our minds enough space and attention to really create and expand, whether it's a question of maths and science or art and philosophy. We *know* we come up with better answers when we have time to think – but more and more we've deprioritised the moments we need for asking those questions.

> **Life is very short and anxious for those who forget the past, neglect the present, and fear the future.**
> — SENECA

Recently I was riding my bike home, pedalling slowly up a hill, when a young guy started trying to talk to me, shouting something I couldn't quite make out. I was still moving, although slowly, so I tried just waving to him to let him know I couldn't hear him. He was still shouting to me, more and more aggressively, but grad-ually I pulled away and he fell behind, giving up his attempt at communication. It was only in the moments after that I realised he was actually trying to mug me.

I've been mugged before and got into a few fights as a kid. The feelings after each one of those events had stayed with me for days, weeks, even months after, the dread of the violence, the fear of another potential attack. But this time, I had no adrenaline, I wasn't shaking, and I went to bed that night with no sense of delayed shock. It struck me that this was Stoicism in action.

I know I'd still be terrified if I opened my front door and there was a massive lion in the front garden because that would represent a real and present danger. But over the years I've studied it, Stoic philosophy has shaped my brain. I realised that day on the bike that I'd lost the habit of seeing danger everywhere, and I only reacted now to 'real' threats, not just those I imagined or projected into potentially dangerous situations. As a teenager, I was just as afraid of social events as I was of fights, terrified of what I imagined I might say, or what someone else might do. And a few years ago, I might have seen the young guy walking along the road and thought, 'He could be a mugger, I'd better move faster,' and arrived home sweating and shaken. But now, even with him attempting to mug me, I hadn't seen any sign of violence or threat, so my brain simply hadn't offered up any alarm. These days, many of my fears have disappeared because the vast majority of my previous fears simply weren't 'real'. You can't think away a truly dangerous situation, but you can let your brain know, moment by moment, that many things we fear don't deserve those feelings – talking to a stranger, going to an interview, travelling somewhere new. And lessening the fear in any of our lives is a worthy goal.

Remind yourself that past and future have no power over you.
— MARCUS AURELIUS

We've all had the experience of being with a group of friends and gradually everyone ends up on their phones. Someone just checks a message, then someone gets their phone out because they're waiting for a reply, then someone else has theirs out to show a TikTok or an Instagram account. Suddenly everyone is hunched over their phones, no one is making eye contact or sharing spontaneous jokes or conversation about the moment they're in – they're just sharing other people's moments and jokes. Will we look back on those times together with our friends and be glad? Or should we make the decision now to enjoy the moments of really being with our friends – no disruptions, just existing together with each other in a way that isn't possible with distance, devices or distractions?

Remember how intense positive moments felt when you were little? As children, we mostly had no huge list of responsibilities or tasks; we could exist in the moment, laughing with our friends, standing in rainstorms, running to something, totally removed from yesterday's memories and tomorrow's burdens. Now, we have bills and jobs, plans and regrets, unfulfilled to-do lists and snoozed reminders, and we tie ourselves so tightly to the present moment with everything past and everything still to come that we can't appreciate anything about the moment we're in. It's like the experience of travelling to another country for a holiday. There's the inevitable stress when we arrive at the destination airport of collecting our bags, queuing for passport control and passing through the customs gates, checking and rechecking that we have everything with us, getting transport to our hotel, checking again that we have all our suitcases and hand luggage, perhaps another bag of things we've picked up in the airport shops too. We reach the hotel and check in, are shown up to our room and can finally put all of our bags down, breathe out, and become aware of our surroundings. Looking out of the hotel window, we're suddenly aware of the weather outside, the buildings next door, the music that was playing in the lobby while we checked in but didn't have the headspace to hear. We can admire the light in our room, the colour on the walls that we don't use as much in our climate, the ocean view. It's the same feeling when we can finally put down the baggage of past and future. Our minds can relax and simply enjoy the moment we're in.

When I was working in construction in my teens, I was living with the constant state of mind 'I can't wait for today to be over.' I was always waiting for the end of the day, living for the weekend. My boss would always say his favourite part of the week was when the radio went off on a Friday, signalling that the week was over and the weekend was finally beginning. The trouble was, there was only a tiny fraction of every week that was the Friday we were all looking forward to – even Friday itself wasn't what I wanted, because most of it was still spent working, then there was the hassle of making plans, then the night would come to an end, and I would have to say goodbye to my friends and get home. Really, there was only an hour or two where I'd actually be enjoying myself and, even then, I had the tiredness from work hanging over me, and the encroaching thought that the weekend would soon be over.

Once I became conscious of it, I gradually realised what a self-defeating habit it was. I wasn't celebrating the weekend, I was constantly grieving it; I wasn't giving myself something to keep me going, I was trapping myself in a negative cycle of unhappiness and regret. I started seeing it everywhere: in ads and on TV, telling us all that we should live for Fridays, for the weekend, for summer, for our holidays. But if we're all rushing towards that one particular day or week or fortnight, that tiny percentage of our life, how can we possibly feel good? If we tell ourselves over and over again that only that one small bit is worth doing, we wish away the majority of the millions of moments we live through. I'd been wishing away the present in the hopes of having a future I'd be more grateful for, but when I got to the 'future', I'd developed such a strong habit of never enjoying the present that I couldn't even find pleasure when I got there. (Later, I got a job cleaning the properties of substance abusers, where the homes had been trashed and left filthy. I enjoyed every day of that work, and fully appreciated the present moment of each task there. It was a delight to realise that I didn't have to wish the day away.)

The time to enjoy our life is now. We don't have to wait for the weekend to enjoy a sunset – the sun sets every single day, after all, and we don't even have to climb a mountain; a Tesco car park, believe it or not, is usually pretty great thanks to its wide-open space and low surrounding roofs – or to call a friend, or make our favourite drink or play the song that always makes us dance. We don't even have to wait for a free day. I've been more than guilty of seeing it's already 7 o'clock in the evening and writing off the rest of the day, saying, 'Oh, I'll do it all properly tomorrow.' The day is not over just because our work day is. We have time now! There are still precious hours in our day that we can use to find the small pleasures that make each day positive, and there are still a million different ways we can remove the attachments of past and future from the present to enjoy this moment in all its glory, achieving a euphoric clarity away from the past and future. And I still struggle – these days, I find it hard to separate a beautiful moment from turning it into a lesson to learn from. Standing in a thunderstorm recently, smelling the rain, feeling it on my skin, watching the lightning above me, I knew that although I'd managed a few moments of enjoyment, my brain was mostly taking it in as a memory to use in a story about living in the moment. But even in those quiet, dull moments that no one would deem perfect enough to put on film or write a song about, we still exist, perfectly.

And the 'perfect time' is never perfect anyway. Every holiday has boring moments, every weekend has chores, every party has a spilled drink or bad song. But if we can find the truth and the enjoyment of Right Now, which is, after all, all we ever have, we can unlock limitless discovery and happiness.

IN SUMMARY

Give up regrets of the past and worries of the future. Enjoy the wonder of the world and be present in this moment.

Your Onward Path

So, you've got this far, and spent your time reading this book. Where do you go from here?

Stoicism is a guide to the good life, the blueprint for becoming the best version of yourself and a practical way to help others. The practical part is the most important – there's no point learning all about Stoicism if you don't incorporate these things into your life. It doesn't have to be all at once, but even a single step is one step on the path to eudaimonia. Acting on your new knowledge makes you a Stoic, and not acting means missing the point – and the joys – of Stoicism.

For thousands of years, Stoics have developed these simple ideas, passing them down through generations and surviving threats from the powerful and from other philosophies, as Stoicism has been translated and transported across the world. From the great emperor Marcus Aurelius, who faced wars and empires, family issues and his own temperament, all the way to you, holding this book in your hands, facing climate change and economic uncertainty, family issues and your own temperament, times change so much and yet not at all. We are all human; we all face problems, challenges, difficulties; we all have the same potential.

While the teachings of Stoicism may be thousands of years old, the problems we face in modern society can still be addressed with this ancient philosophy. Humans have created the problems of internet noise, smartphone distraction, a culture of consumption and attention, and humans can solve them through implementing the Four Virtues into our everyday lives to offer us the space in our minds to exist in peace and contentment. We all want to enjoy a world of truth, fairness, honesty, responsibility and kindness, and to live free from fear.

*

I hope this book helps you to discover, and to build, that better world.

The Stoic Life

Be present. Accept that the only thing that exists is this very moment right here.

Focus solely on things within your control. Free yourself from the burden of desiring and comparing.

Shape your actions around the Four Virtues. Aim towards truth and balance, fairness and courage.

Feel gratitude for what you have now. Remember death, and that all of us are equal and have a fair passage to eudaimonia.

Be mindful of your thoughts. Claim your power to stand up and be the good in the world.

Text Sources

p.24 'One isn't necessarily born with courage . . .' Maya Angelou, *USA Today*, 5 March 1988.

p.58 'we're all unhappier, more anxious, more depressed . . .' *Hidden Brain* podcast, 'The Paradox of Pleasure' episode, 39.03.

p.78 'Most of our pain, most of our suffering comes from resistance . . .' Michael Sandler, *Inspire Nation Show*, 'Love Yourself Like Your Life Depends on It', Kamal Ravikant Power Life-Changing interview, 23.06.

p.88 'In the midst of winter, I found there was . . .' Albert Camus, 'Return to Tipasa', collected in *Summer*.

p.88 'The darker the night, the brighter the stars.' Fyodor Dostoyevsky, *Crime and Punishment*.

p.110 'when you are dancing . . .' Alan Watts, *The Wisdom of Insecurity*.

p.114 'It is not daily increase but daily decrease . . .' Bruce Lee / Bruce Lee Enterprises LLC.

p.115 'God, give me the serenity to accept the things I cannot change . . .' Reinhold Niebuhr, Serenity Prayer.

p.158 'the profound feeling of realising that everyone, including strangers . . .' John Koenig, *The Dictionary of Obscure Sorrows*, Simon & Schuster LLC © 2021 John Koenig.

p.164 'People really are the same everywhere . . .' Ryan Holiday, *Daily Stoic*.

p.176 'When I was a boy and I would see scary things in the news . . .' *Television Academy Foundation*, 'Fred Rogers Interview', interviewed

by Karen Herman, 22 July 1999. Visit https://
protect-eu.mimecast.com/s/xoHlCJy8xfro
xO9CVWIXW?domain=televisionacademy.
com"TelevisionAcademy.com/interviews for
more information.

p.202 'People often avoid the truth for fear of
destroying . . .' Joshua Fields Milburn and Ryan
Nicodemus, *Everything That Remains: A Memoir by
The Minimalists*.

p.248 'Your need for acceptance can make
you invisible in this world . . .' Jim Carrey,
Commencement Speech at the Maharishi
University of Management, https://www.
youtube.com/watch?v=V80-gPkpH6M.

p.266 'What makes it unbearable is your mistaken
belief that it can be cured.' Charlotte Joko Beck.

p.266 'Suffering is not an anomaly but a clue to
freeing the mind . . .' John Tarrant, 'Hidden In
Plain Sight', 1 May 2015.